PEASANT COOKING
OF MANY LANDS

BY CORALIE CASTLE & MARGARET GIN
HISTORICAL TEXT BY ALFRED E. CASTLE
DRAWINGS BY WILLIAM GIN
101 PRODUCTIONS   SAN FRANCISCO   1972

Library of Congress Catalog Card Number 72-77566

Distributed to the Book Trade in the United States of America
by Charles Scribner's Sons, New York

Distributed in Canada by Van Nostrand Reinhold Ltd.

PUBLISHED BY 101 PRODUCTIONS
79 Liberty Street, San Francisco, California 94110

INTRODUCTION

T HIS BOOK is no less than man's culinary history; it is also, in gratuitous spinoff, both a mirror of man's soul and a partial guide to the evolution of human consciousness. Man reaches out—that is history. The Pacific link is now forged between West and East. The pageant of forming this great human circle is no better illustrated by its messiahs, conquerors, queens, generals, statesmen and scientists than it is by those who harmonize with the soil cycles and who pursue the time-honored crafts. Food, of course, is central to the design of peasant cultures.

Some of the recipes which follow are thousands of years old; many developed during the Middle Ages; some are only of a couple or few centuries' standing. Nevertheless, all of these classical dishes are still contemporary standards within their native cuisines. Characteristic of the facility with which we transmit information in today's ever-accelerating environment, we can all now enjoy peasant cooking of many lands.

CONTENTS

 Many recipes in this book call for ingredients marked with an asterisk. Explanations of these ingredients are found in the glossary on pages 183-185.

BASICS

BASICS

GENERAL RULES FOR MAKING BREAD

• Flour differs in batches and in various locales, so approximate measurements are given. When kneading dough, use enough flour to form an elastic, smooth dough which no longer sticks to your fingers. Always knead *at least* 10 minutes; you can't knead too long.

• Yeast is given in tablespoon measurements because we recommend active dry yeast available in natural food stores in bulk. When dissolving, use lukewarm water from the tap (105°- 110°) and let yeast bubble slightly before proceeding.

• To let rise: form a ball of dough, rub lightly with oil, place in bowl and cover bowl with a damp tea towel. Set aside in a warm place, (80° - 85°), free of drafts, and let stand until doubled in bulk. The time depends upon the type of bread.

• When baking in Pyrex pans, lower given oven temperature by 25°.

• After baking cool bread on rack.

• If crusty bread is desired, put a pan of water on bottom rack of oven or brush top of bread with a little water before baking. If less crust is desired place a dry tea towel over loaf immediately after turning out onto rack after baking.

PAIN ORDINAIRE
French Bread—Basic White

Dissolve in:
1/2 cup warm water
2 tablespoons dry yeast
Add:
2 teaspoons salt
1-1/2 cups warm water
Gradually work in:
**about 5-1/2 cups
  unbleached flour**
Turn out on floured board and knead until elastic and smooth. Let rise until double in bulk, turn out on floured board and knead briefly. Shape into 2 long loaves tapering at ends. Place on greased cookie sheet and let rise for 45 minutes. Cut 3 diagonal slashes on loaves, brush with water and bake in a 375° oven 30 minutes until golden.
Makes 2 loaves

NAN
Pakistani Bread

Make half of preceding recipe for Pain Ordinaire, using whole wheat flour instead of unbleached. After first rising, form 12 balls. Roll each 1/4-inch thick, let rise 15 minutes, turn over onto greased baking sheet and bake in a 500° oven about 10 minutes. Watch carefully so they do not brown too much.

BAGELS

Make half of preceding recipe for Pain Ordinaire, adding with yeast:
2 tablespoons sugar
**1/2-1 cup finely minced onions
  (optional)**
**1/3 cup poppy seeds or caraway
  seeds (optional)**
After first rising, knead briefly and form into balls, flat rounds or rings. Boil in rapidly boiling salted water until they rise to top, drain and place on greased cookie sheet. Bake in a 425° oven 25-30 minutes until crusty and golden.
Makes 24

PITA
Flat Bread

Make half of preceding recipe for Pain Ordinaire. Follow preceding directions for Nan.

GRISSINI
Italian Bread Sticks

Make half of preceding recipe for Pain Ordinaire. After first rising, roll into ropes and form sticks 6 to 8-inches long, about 3/4-inch in diameter.
Roll in:
sesame seeds
poppy seeds or
coarse salt
Bake in a 400° oven
10-15 minutes until golden.
Makes about 2-1/2 dozen

CORNMEAL
Mamaliga, Polenta

Combine in a large saucepan:
1 quart water
1 teaspoon salt
1 cup yellow cornmeal
Bring to boil, stirring constantly over medium heat until very thick (5 minutes or so). Lower heat to simmer, cover and cook 15 minutes. Turn out on board or platter and form into desired shape.
Serves 4

SWEDISH-ONION
RYE BREAD

Dissolve in:
1 cup warm water
1 tablespoon dry yeast
Scald:
1 cup milk
Add and cool to lukewarm:
2 tablespoons each butter
   and sugar
1 teaspoon salt
Add to yeast with:
3/4 cup finely minced onion
1/4 cup caraway seeds
about 3 cups each unbleached
   flour and rye flour
Turn out on rye-floured board and knead until elastic and smooth. Let rise 1-1/2 hours, punch down, knead briefly and shape into 2 round loaves. Place on greased baking sheet and let rise until double. Bake in a 400° oven 35 minutes.
Makes 2 loaves

BASICS

CHALLAH
Egg Bread

Dissolve in:
2 cups warm water
2 tablespoons dry yeast
Add and mix well:
1 tablespoon salt
1/2 cup sugar
3/4 cup corn oil
4 eggs, beaten
4 cups unbleached flour
1/2 cup soy flour
Gradually add:
about 3 cups unbleached flour
Turn out on floured board and knead until elastic and smooth. Let rise until double, about 1-1/2 hours, punch down, knead briefly and shape into 3 loaves. Place in 3 greased loaf pans and let rise 1 hour. Brush with:
beaten egg yolk
Bake in a 350° oven 45 minutes or until golden.
Makes 3 loaves

PEASANT BREAD
Central Europe

Boil in water to cover:
3 medium potatoes
Save water, peel the potatoes and mash while still hot.
Dissolve in:
1/2 cup warm potato water
1 tablespoon dry yeast
Add and combine well:
2 cups of the mashed potatoes
2 cups reserved warm potato water
2 teaspoons salt
2 tablespoons each softened butter and dark molasses
2 tablespoons anise, fennel, dill or caraway seeds
2 cups each rye flour, whole wheat flour and unbleached flour
Beat well and turn out on rye-floured board, adding more rye flour as needed. Knead until elastic and smooth. Let rise until double, about 1-1/2 hours, punch down and knead briefly. Shape into 2 round loaves, place on greased baking sheet and let rise until double. Bake in a 400° oven 40 minutes.
Makes 2 loaves

BASIC SWEET BREAD DOUGH

Scald and then cool to lukewarm:
1 cup milk
Dissolve in:
1/2 cup warm water
2 tablespoons yeast
Add scalded milk and:
1/2 cup sugar
1 teaspoon salt
1/2 cup softened butter
5 eggs, beaten
1 teaspoon each vanilla and freshly grated lemon rind
about 5 cups unbleached flour
Turn out on floured board and knead until elastic and smooth. Let rise until double, about 1-1/2 hours, punch down, knead briefly and shape as directed in individual recipes. Bake as directed.

SOURDOUGH BREAD

Add to:
1 cup starter
1 cup each lukewarm water and unbleached flour
Let stand at room temperature for at least 8 hours. Then add:
about 2 cups unbleached flour
Knead until smooth, form into ball, place in oiled bowl, spread oil on top, cover with tea towel and let rise until double in bulk (1-1/2 to 2 hours depending upon sourness of the dough). Punch down and let rest 10 minutes. Shape into a round loaf, place on greased baking sheet and let rise until double in bulk. Bake in a 400° oven 25 minutes.
Makes 1 loaf

SOURDOUGH STARTER

Boil until soft in:
3 cups water
1 medium potato, peeled
Mash with 2 cups of potato liquid and cool to lukewarm. Then add and dissolve thoroughly:
1 tablespoon dry yeast
Place in earthenware bowl, cover lightly, and let stand at room temperature for 3 days. Blend in:
1 cup each unbleached flour and lukewarm water
Let stand at room temperature another 24 hours. Starter is now ready to use. To store, cover and refrigerate. If not using every week discard 1/2 cup starter and replace with:
1/2 cup each unbleached flour and lukewarm water
If using, replace with amount taken out for particular recipe. Let stand at room temperature 24 hours, cover and refrigerate.

OATMEAL CINNAMON RAISIN LOAF

Make **Oatmeal Bread** (page 10); after first rising knead in:
1 cup raisins
Divide dough in half, roll out 1/4-inch thick and spread each half with:
1 tablespoon softened butter
1/4 cup sugar
1/2 teaspoon cinnamon
Roll up like jelly roll and place in greased bread pans. Let rise until double and bake in a 375° oven 35-40 minutes.
Makes 2 loaves

BASICS

POTATO BREAD

In water to cover cook
until soft:
3 medium potatoes
Reserve water, peel potatoes
and mash while still hot.
Dissolve in:
1/2 cup warm potato water
2 tablespoons dry yeast
Add:
2 cups of the mashed potatoes
1-1/2 cups warm potato water
2 tablespoons butter or lard
2 teaspoons salt
2 tablespoons sugar
**about 5-1/2 cups unbleached
    flour**
Turn out on board, knead until
elastic and smooth and let rise
until double, about 1-1/2 hours,
punch down, knead briefly and
shape into 3 loaves. Place on
greased baking sheet, let rise
until double and bake in
a 375° oven 40 minutes. Or
make 2 loaves and a pan of rolls.
(Pinch off small pieces of dough,
place in a greased 9-inch square
pan and bake 20 minutes.)
Light in texture, and moist.

OATMEAL BREAD

Combine:
1 cup scalded milk
1 cup boiling water
1/3 cup honey
2 tablespoons butter
Add and let stand 1/2 hour:
2 cups rolled oats
2 teaspoons salt
Dissolve in:
1/4 cup warm water
1 tablespoon dry yeast
Add to oatmeal mixture and
blend well. Then add:
1 cup oat flour
**about 3-1/2 cups unbleached
    flour**
Turn out on floured board and
knead until elastic and smooth.
Let rise until double, about 1-1/2
hours, punch down and knead
briefly. Let rest 10 minutes,
shape into 2 loaves and place in
greased bread pans. Let rise
until double and bake in a
375° oven 40 minutes.
Makes 2 loaves

BROA
Cornbread

Combine and let stand until
lukewarm:
1-1/2 cups yellow cornmeal
1 teaspoon salt
1-1/2 cups boiling water
1 tablespoon olive oil
Dissolve in:
1 tablespoon dry yeast
1 teaspoon sugar
Add to cornmeal mixture and
blend in:
about 2-1/2 cups unbleached flour
Turn out on floured board and
knead until smooth and elastic.
Let rise until double, about 1-1/2
hours, and form into 1 large
round loaf. Place on greased
baking sheet, let rise again,
and bake in a 400° oven
30 minutes.
Makes 1 loaf

NOODLE DOUGH

Sift onto large board:
3-1/2 cups unbleached flour
1 teaspoon salt
Make hollow in center and add:
5 eggs
1 tablespoon oil
With fingers, using spatula to bring flour from edges, gradually blend eggs and oil into flour. Knead gently until dough no longer sticks to fingers, adding more flour as needed. When thoroughly blended and smooth form into a ball, cover with dampened towel and let rest 20 minutes. Divide into 6 equal portions and roll each out as thinly as possible, using flour as needed. Place each sheet on floured wax paper and let dry only as long as it takes to roll entire batch. Starting with first sheet, roll half nearest you away from you like a jelly roll, then roll half farthest from you toward center like a jelly roll to meet in center. With very sharp knife cut into desired widths; with blunt edge of knife lift at center fold and shake strips free. Hang over back of chair only until all dough is used. If not cooking within 10 minutes, lay strips on floured wax paper, roll up and seal, using more flour if needed to prevent strips from sticking together. Or place on floured cookie sheets, freeze and wrap. Refrigerate several hours. Makes about 2 pounds, enough for 8 servings

GREEN NOODLES

Sift onto large bread board:
3 cups unbleached flour
1 teaspoon salt
Make hollow in center and break into it:
3 eggs
Follow above directions; when almost blended knead in:
1/2 cup finely minced cooked spinach, squeezed dry
Makes a little over 1 pound

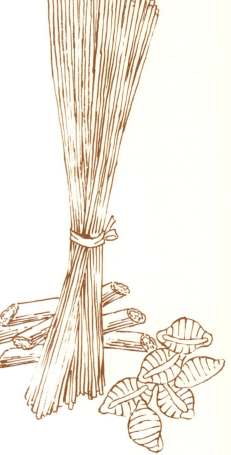

BASICS

CHINESE NOODLES**

Break into measuring cup:
1 egg
Add:
1 teaspoon oil and
   enough water to bring
   measurement to 1/2 cup
   + 2 tablespoons
Sift together:
2 cups unbleached flour
1 teaspoon salt
Add egg and water, mix well and
turn out on floured board. Knead
until smooth, using more flour
only if needed. Cover with
dampened cloth and let rest
20 minutes. Follow directions
for basic noodles.
Makes 1 pound

WONTONS **

These are called **molo** in the
Philippines.
Make Chinese noodle dough.
Divide dough into 4 equal parts.
Roll each into a 9-inch length
rope, wrap in wax paper and
refrigerate 20 minutes. Cut off
1-inch pieces, roll each into
a 4-inch square or circle,
stacking as you go along. Keep
wontons covered.
Makes 36; with noodle
machine, 48

EGG ROLL SKINS**

Follow above directions. Roll
each division of dough into
a 4-inch length rope. Cut off
1-inch pieces and roll into
4 7-inch rounds or squares.
Makes 28; with noodle
machine, 32

**Fresh noodles can be purchased
in Oriental markets, as can the
wonton and **egg roll skins,**
either in squares or rounds.
Inexpensive and thinner.

BASIC METHOD OF COOKING NOODLES AND ALL PASTA

For each pound of fresh noodles
or 12 ounces of dried:
Bring to boil:
2 quarts water
2 tablespoons salt
3 tablespoons oil
Gradually add noodles and boil
over medium heat, stirring
occasionally, 3 minutes for
fresh, about 8 for dried; cook
only until *just* tender
(al dente)—do not overcook.
Lift from pot with fork and put
into bowl with:
2 tablespoons butter
   or olive oil
Or merely dress with more butter
or oil, grated Parmesan cheese
and black pepper; add cream
if desired.

PASTRY CRUST

For tender crust, handle dough as little as possible. Blend dough ingredients, form in ball and roll out.

HOT WATER PASTRY

Beat until smooth and creamy:
**1 cup pork lard*, lard
   or shortening**
Beat in until well blended:
**1/3 cup boiling water
1 tablespoon milk**
Sift together and add:
**2-1/2 cups unbleached flour
1 teaspoon salt**
Makes 2 crusts
Note: An electric mixer works well in blending lard and liquids.
Lower heat and gradually add egg mixture. Cook and stir until slightly thickened. Toss the greens which have been torn or cut into 2-inch lengths and transfer to salad bowl. Garnish with sliced hard-cooked eggs.

CREAM CHEESE PASTRY

Sift together:
**1 cup + 2 tablespoons
   unbleached flour
3/4 teaspoon salt**
Cut in:
**4 tablespoons butter
1 3-ounce package cream cheese**
Mix in:
1 egg, beaten
Makes 1 crust

BISCUIT PASTRY DOUGH

Sift together:
**1 cup unbleached flour
2 teaspoons baking powder
1/2 teaspoon salt**
Mix in:
**1 egg, beaten
2 tablespoons each softened
   butter and corn oil**
If too stiff add a little cold water.
Makes 1 crust

Note: If doubling this recipe, double all ingredients except baking powder.

CRÊPES

Beat together:
**4 eggs
1 cup sifted unbleached flour
1/4 teaspoon salt
1 tablespoon oil
1-1/3 cups milk**
Cover and refrigerate at least 2 hours.
Heat a 7-inch crêpe pan, butter lightly and when butter bubbles pour in 3 tablespoons of batter. Quickly tip the pan from side to side to coat entire bottom. Cook until golden over medium heat; turn and cook other side 1 minute. While cooking crêpes, stir batter often, adding more milk if too thick. As each crêpe is cooked, place it on a rack set on a cookie sheet and cover with an inverted bowl. Keep warm in a slow oven if using immediately; otherwise keep covered at room temperature until ready to use.
Makes 20 crêpes

BASICS

RICE-COOKING METHODS

- **General** Unless otherwise specified, white rice should be long-grain variety. Plan 1/3 cup rice per person. To wash place in pan, rinse, rub briskly with fingers and pour off water. Repeat until water is clear. Pan should be at least double the raw rice capacity and should have a tight-fitting lid.
- **Chinese Method** Level washed rice in pan and add water to cover 1/2 inch above rice layer. Let stand at least 30 minutes or longer. Over high heat, uncovered, bring to rapid boil, lower heat slightly and cook until *all* the water has evaporated and bubbles have disappeared. Cover tightly, reduce heat immediately to lowest point, and cook 20 minutes. Any crust that may have formed on bottom may be eaten like bread; or water can be added to make rice tea.
- **Japanese Method** Wash *short* grain (pearl) rice (it's much starchier and needs more changes of water). Soak in water to cover 30 minutes or until grains appear milky white. Drain. Bring equal measurement of water to boil and gradually stir in rice.

Cover tightly and cook on high heat until rice starts to steam over; turn heat to medium and cook 6 minutes. Turn off heat and let stand 20 minutes.
- **Greek Method (Pilaf)** In 3 tablespoons butter or olive oil, cook and stir 2 cups washed and well-drained rice and the sieved pulp of 2 ripe tomatoes. Add 4 cups water and 1/2 teaspoon salt. Bring to boil, lower heat, cover and simmer 20 minutes. Remove lid and wipe off any moisture that has collected; gently stir 1 tablespoon finely minced fresh basil into rice, and cover. Let stand on lowest heat until rice is dry and flaky. Serves 4-6
- **Turkish Method (Pilau)** In 3 tablespoons oil cook and stir 2 cups washed and well-drained rice, 2 tablespoons pine nuts and 1/2 cup finely minced onion until rice is just golden. Add 4 cups boiling water, sieved pulp of 3 ripe tomatoes, 1/2 teaspoon each salt and allspice, 1/4 teaspoon black pepper and 2-3 tablespoons currants (soaked to soften, then dried). Bring to boil, cover and cook over lowest heat 20-30 minutes. Serves 4-6

- **Brown Rice** Wash and soak the rice in water to cover 2 hours before draining and cooking by any basic method.
- **Wild Rice Substitute** Use half white and half soaked and drained brown rice.
- **Italian Method (Risotto)** Soften 1/2 cup dried mushrooms in 1 cup of warm water. Strain, reserve liquid, dice mushrooms and set aside. Brown 1/4 cup diced onion, 1 minced garlic clove and 1-1/4 cups washed and drained rice in 4 tablespoons butter. Heat liquid from mushrooms with 3 cups chicken stock and add to rice a cup at a time. After each addition cover and cook until liquid is absorbed. Add mushrooms with second cup. Continue until all stock is used; add 1/3 cup sherry or Madeira in which 1/4 teaspoon saffron has been dissolved. Cook until liquid is absorbed. With fork toss in 2 tablespoons softened butter and season to taste with salt and pepper. Serve with a generous amount of grated Parmesan cheese. If stickier rice is desired, use 1 cup more liquid and cook rice uncovered. Serves 4

- **Burmese Method (Ohm Htamin)** Sauté 1 finely chopped onion in 2 tablespoons oil until soft. Add 2 cups washed and drained rice and brown until just golden. Add 1 teaspoon salt, 1 cup coconut milk (page 17) and 1-1/2 cups water or enough to cover leveled rice with 1/2 inch of liquid. Bring to boil, stir gently, cover and simmer over low heat 20 minutes or until moisture is absorbed.
Serves 6
- **Iranian Method (Chelou)** Wash and soak 2 cups rice (preferably imported Persian rice available in specialty shops) in 1 tablespoon salt and enough water to cover for 1 hour or more. Drain and gradually add to 8 cups boiling water and 1-1/2 tablespoons salt. Boil rapidly, uncovered, for 10 minutes, drain and rinse in hot water. Mix with 1/3 cup milk. Melt 4 tablespoons butter and 2 tablespoons water in heavy deep saucepan. Tip pan to coat sides then cover bottom with 1-1/2 cups of the cooked rice and milk. Mound remaining rice in center of pan, patting edges to hold mound in shape. With handle of wooden spoon make a hole in center almost to

bottom of pan, cover tightly and bake in a 375° oven 15 minutes. Reduce heat to 350° and sprinkle rice with 2 tablespoons hot water and 1/4 cup melted butter. Cover and bake on lowest rack of oven 50 minutes. Let stand on cool surface 15 minutes, turn out onto large heated platter and form mound. Scrape crust from bottom and arrange around rice. Make a hollow in center of mound and break into it 1 or 2 egg yolks. Sprinkle all with salt and black pepper and garnish with parsley.
Serves 6
- **Bulgarian Method** Sauté 1/2 cup chopped onions, 1 minced garlic clove, 2-3 hot chili peppers (page 17) and 2 cups washed and drained rice in 2 tablespoons pork lard* until rice is golden. Add 4 cups water or stock and 1/2 teaspoon salt. Bring to boil, cover and simmer 20 minutes until rice is fluffy and dry.
Serves 6
- **Puerto Rican Method (Arroz) Sofrito** Sauté 1 finely chopped bell pepper, 1 diced onion and 1/4 cup chopped cilantro* in 1/3 cup oil 5 minutes. Add 2 pressed garlic cloves, 1 teaspoon crushed fresh oregano, 1 8-ounce

can tomato sauce, 1/2 cup pimiento-stuffed olives, sliced, 1 tablespoon capers and salt and pepper to taste. Cover and simmer 10 minutes, stirring often. Mix in 2 cups washed and drained rice. Add water to cover rice level by 1/2 inch, stir, bring to boil and over medium heat cook until moisture has evaporated. Turn to lowest heat, cover and cook 20-30 minutes.
Serves 6
- **Brazilian Method** Sauté 1 finely chopped onion and 1 minced garlic clove until soft in 2 tablespoons oil. Add 1 cup chopped fresh tomatoes, 1 cup washed and drained rice, 1/2 teaspoon salt, 1/4 teaspoon pepper and 1-1/2 cups water. Bring to boil, lower heat to medium and cook until all bubbles have evaporated. Cover and cook over low heat 20 minutes.
Serves 4
- **Peruvian Method** Cook 1 pressed garlic clove, covered, in 2 tablespoons olive oil. Add 4 cups water, 1-2 tablespoons lemon juice and 1/2 teaspoon salt. Bring to boil and gradually add 2 cups washed rice. Cover and simmer 20-30 minutes.
Serves 4-6

15

BASICS

STOCKS

• **Lamb, Pork, Beef, Veal, Poultry and Game Stocks** may be made from fresh bones or leftovers. For every pound of bones use a quart of cold water. Bring slowly to boil, skim off any scum that rises to the top, cover and simmer 2 to 3 hours for fresh bones, 2 hours for leftovers. Bones may be browned before boiling. Pigs' feet, marrow and knuckle bones (blanch first), vegetables and scrapings, water in which vegetables have been cooked, herbs and seasonings—all may be added at will.

• **Chinese** stocks are made with fresh, unbrowned chicken or pork bones; then simmered 1 or 2 hours and salted to taste. A slice of ginger may be added.

• **Japanese** basic stock, Dashi, is given on page 33.

• **Court Bouillon** Sauté 1/2 cup mixed vegetables such as leeks, onion, celery and carrot in 2 tablespoons butter until soft. Add 1 quart water, 1 pound fish heads and/or scraps, 6 parsley sprigs, 6 peppercorns, 1 bay leaf, 2 thyme sprigs, 1 teaspoon salt and 2 tablespoons lemon juice. Bring to boil, skim off any scum that rises to surface, cover and simmer 20 minutes—no longer. Strain. Can omit lemon juice and substitute 2 cups dry white wine for 2 cups of the water.

• **To Store Stocks** Sieve into jars, cool and refrigerate. The fat on top (except with dashi) will keep the stock fresh up to a week. If not using within that time, remove from refrigerator, bring back to boil, cool and store again.

EGG GARNI

Beat together:
4 eggs
2 tablespoons water
1/4 teaspoon salt
Add to heavy heated skillet:
1 teaspoon corn oil
Heat oil and pour in half the egg mixture. Cook over medium heat until set. Turn out on cutting board and repeat with rest of eggs. Cool, roll and slice thinly.

HOT SALAD DRESSING

For dandelion greens, spinach, watercress, iceberg or Romaine lettuce, cabbage.

Beat together:
1 egg
1 tablespoon sugar
2 tablespoons each vinegar and water
Dice and fry until crisp:
3 slices bacon

BASIC HINTS

• **Boiling Salted Water** Use 1 teaspoon salt to 2 quarts of water; if adding lemon, 2 tablespoons to 2 quarts.

• **Testing Cakes and Custards** Toothpick inserted in center should come out clean.

• **Legumes** Pick over and wash before soaking or using.

• **Vegetables** Cooking time depends upon age and freshness; save cooking water for stock.

• **Pepper and Nutmeg** Use freshly ground.

• **Cheese** Whenever possible, specified types of cheese should be from the country of origin. Grated cheese should always be freshly grated.

- **Herbs** Unless otherwise specified recipes use dried herbs. Fresh are far superior, however; triple measurement if substituting fresh.
- **Soy Sauce** Use the Japanese variety which is lighter and less salty.
- **Pyrex** Lower oven temperature by 25° if using Pyrex baking dishes.
- **Oven Temperature** Always preheat oven.
- **Eggs** All recipes call for grade A large.
- **Rendered Fat** Chicken, pork, ham or beef. Melt minced fat over medium heat, cool, pour into container and refrigerate or freeze. Cracklings are good in biscuits or as toppings for soups and stews.
- **Paprika** Imported Hungarian recommended; sold in Middle Eastern stores.
- **Hot Chilis** Be careful in handling. The vein and seeds are the hottest part. If a hotter taste is desired do not discard seeds and veins when adding to a recipe.
- **To Plump Raisins** Soak in warm water to cover 30 minutes.
- **To Make Coconut Milk** Bring 1 cup unsweetened grated coconut* and 1 cup milk to a boil. Remove from heat, cool and sieve. Use as directed. Repeat process if less concentrated milk is desired. To substitute add 1/2 teaspoon coconut extract to 1 cup milk.
- **Binding** Mix together 1 tablespoon cornstarch, arrowroot or tapioca flour; 1/4 cup cold water and 1/8 teaspoon salt. Gradually add to pan juices for desired thickness the last minute of cooking; cook and stir until translucent and just thickened.
- **Stir frying** Heat a skillet or wok very hot; add amount of oil indicated and heat to sizzling. Add ingredients, cook and stir quickly following recipe directions. The secret is quick cooking to retain flavor and crispness.
- **To Marinate** Never use a metal container.
- **Using a Steamer** Place ingredients in a shallow bowl in which the dish is to be served—*not* plastic or aluminum. Place bowl on a rack in a steamer or kettle large enough so bowl can be lifted out easily. Fill kettle with 1-1/2 inches of water, cover tightly and bring to boil. Steam over medium heat the stated amount of time. Two or even three bowls can be stacked by laying chopsticks across bowls to serve as racks.
- **Al Dente** To cook until tender but still firm.
- **Blanch** To parboil for a specified length of time.
- **Deglaze** Pour liquid into pan juices and scrape up all bits.
- **Phyllo** Very thin dough almost impossible to make at home; available in 1-pound packages in Armenian or Greek specialty shops and many delicatessens. If frozen be sure to defrost overnight in the refrigerator. The sheets dry out rapidly and are easily broken. Take out one sheet at a time, reroll the rest and cover with a damp towel. To spread with melted butter use a soft brush (a paint brush works nicely). If sheets break they can be "mended" with another buttered sheet. Work quickly and layer or fold as directed in recipe. If well wrapped, phyllo will keep up to a week in the refrigerator.

FAR EAST

TO SAY that Far East diets consist mostly of rice, spices, fruits, vegetables, chicken, fish, beef, lamb and pork and that the diets vary regionally according to availability and religion is like flying at 40,000 feet observing only mountains, plains, rivers and roads—no people. Subtle specifics, not generalities, are the important things in preparing foods of China, India, Japan, Pakistan, Korea, Burma, Indo-China and Ceylon. Westerners are just now really beginning to appreciate Asian delicacies thousands of years old and are adopting them with gusto.

It's not that the world has been completely unaware of Oriental foods. Epic battles were fought over spices of the Indies, the search for which shaped the course of history. A wild semi-aquatic marsh grass, *oryza sativa*, after turning ancient wandering Bengalis into farmers, has become the world's largest single crop—rice. For centuries its easily digested energy, vital proteins (tryptophan, arginine, histidine) and phosphorus have nourished millions of people.

Asia is a harsh continent. Much of it is barren, and crops are sometimes poor. Where food is easy to grow the population explosion started long ago.

Less civilized peoples faced with hunger and hardship might have reverted to animal ways, but not most Asians. Their harsh existence seems only to have forged a keener determination to turn scarce food into treasures to be served and savored with transcendental artistry and ritual. Even today there is much of the occult in their approach to food, a heritage from the thousands of years during which food preoccupied kings, philosophers, artists, poets and religious messiahs.

Colorful vegetables, translucent shark fins, tantalizing curry fragrances, mysterious spice blends, mixtures of individually distinguishable contrasting ingredients —beautiful, original food arrangements have been Asian peasant fare since earliest recorded history.

In the China of antiquity, as elsewhere, climate, terrain, wild foods, domestication of crops and livestock determined local and regional food styles. Sun-drying, smoking and pickling are important elements in the evolution of Eastern cuisine, just as more efficient transportation and ever-increasing communications with new groups brought new approaches and ingredients into play.

For example, Americans acquainted only with southern-style Cantonese foods like stir-fried rice, egg rolls, egg foo yung or roast pork may be surprised by the northern provinces' great use of wheat flour turned into steamed breads, dumplings and noodles, their mutton and sweet and sour fish, and their great use of wine, garlic and scallions in cooking. Even more startling may be inland Szechwan's fiery, spicy beef, its ox tendon and its duck cooked so thoroughly the bones can be crunched and swallowed.

In China, Japan and Korea the Western order of importance of meat, fowl and fish is reversed to fish, fowl and meat, though the Koreans have fewer fish dishes. Today's American eats an average of 150 pounds of *meat* annually; the Asian 35 pounds. Chinese cuisine is richest, Japanese sweetest, Korean in between. Korean farmers make a dark rice tea by almost burning a little rice left in the pan, then pouring water over and bringing to a boil. They feed their pigs soybeans and leftover food, making pork extra tender and on the lean side. Barbecuing is popular; wild bluebell roots and other "natural" vegetables supplement those grown on the farms. Koreans are avid soup eaters; slurping is acceptable etiquette.

In China ceramic spoons are used as well as chopsticks. Perhaps because their soup is usually thinner, with only a few delicate sippets for decoration, the Japanese use only chopsticks, and they sip directly from the bowl. All three peoples believe metal eating utensils impart an undesirable taste to food, and whether or not this be true, the mastering of chopsticks is worth the effort for it gives Westerners a great sense of accomplishment when small slippery peas are first transported up to the mouth without the chopsticks ignominiously crossing like skis.

Japan's distinctive foods can be attributed to a long period of early isolation from the rest of the world during which it continually refined indigenous styles and dishes. Later, Chinese culture and cuisine were introduced and became well known in Japan from 500 to 800 A.D., but when that contact was broken, the Imperial Court developed its own Golden Age of art and poetry. Still maintaining their basic diet of rice, fish, fruit and vegetables, ceremony and style became so central to the new cuisine that even later, when the peasant-based Samurai warriors came to power, elaborate etiquette remained. The Chinese imported soybean had terrific impact. Not only were they eventually cooked and eaten green or as bean sprouts, but soybeans became the basis for *tofu*, soybean curd; *abura-age*, fried tofu; *natto*, steamed and fermented beans; *miso*, fermented bean paste; and *shoyu*, soy sauce.

Another "opening of the gates" occurred about 1550 when Portuguese sailors arrived and established trade with the Far East. In Japan this commerce lasted only until 1638, not just because the Japanese considered the Portuguese uncouth barbarians, but because the latter started to meddle in politics. They were kicked out and communication with the West ceased for two hundred years, yet we can thank the Portuguese for suggesting delightful *tempura*. The Portuguese custom of eating shrimp dipped in batter, then deep fried in fat at certain holy times (Latin *tempora*) suggested a new dish which the Japanese typically improved by using lighter batter and lighter oil and cooking for a shorter time in the round, shallow Oriental *wok*. We now enjoy delicious tempura vegetables as well as shrimp. The *wok*, along with the bamboo-handle flat wire strainers, large cooking chopsticks and Oriental cleavers are sound additions to any kitchen; their versatility seems unlimited.

Japanese salads are outstanding as another fine example of the light, delicate touch in food, and all types of *sushi*, called by some the Japanese sandwich, prove how endless are the uses of rice. Perhaps the epitome of what is best in the texture, visual beauty and delicate flavor of Japanese food—*sashimi*—has scared off more apple-pie Americans than any other single dish. "Raw fish? - ugh!" quickly can turn to "*Sashimi*! Ahhhh—" if preconceived notions are abandoned and the chef selects only the freshest tuna or bass. A good dipping sauce and the symmetry of the garnishes are essential adjuncts in the succulent display of thinly sliced pink and white slices of fish.

It's quite a jump to India-Pakistan, a subcontinent of curries, chutney and *ghee* (clarified buffalo butter that keeps without refrigeration), whose foods have lost a lot in the translation by the British and other invaders who have come and gone throughout history. In the north, food, like the climate, is drier; vegetables and fruit are sun-dried and there are many wheat "breads" quite different from ours. Nearer the equator and closer to sea level fresh fruits and vegetables abound. There's more rice, and vegetable oils are used more than *ghee*. Religion in India plays a larger part in eating habits than Buddhism does in China. The Muslims eat mostly beef and lamb, while Hindus as vegetarians shun beef. Some of the higher castes even avoid eggs. Eating is done with the fingers, right hand only, the left being considered permanently unclean. A kitchen, even though humble, should have a *chula* (brick and plaster charcoal stove) for cooking, a *chakki* (grindstone of stone dishes) for grinding fresh flour and a stone mortar and pestle for making a special *masala* (freshly ground blended spices, wet or dry, bland or hot) for every curry dish.

In India use of "curry powder" like that of commercial chutney is a sacrilege, because its flavors fade and, worst of all, it cuts the heart out of Indian cooking; the originality and subtle variety which express each cook's creativity. "Curry" is a way of preparing food; "a curry" is an aromatic, savory, finished masterpiece as served; it is not a bottle of spice powder. In south India fresh spices such as leaf coriander, green chilis and ginger can be bought as required from spice vendors. Otherwise, jars of dry cinnamon, cardamom, cloves, saffron, turmeric and ginger root, black pepper, cumin, coriander seed and chilis are kept on the shelf along with others filled with soft vegetable pickles in brine, harder ones in oil.

From India's Malabar coast and the Spice Islands, Java, Sumatra, the Celebes and the Moluccas, spices were spread by Phoenicians of King Solomon's court, later by land caravans and sea traders. These exotic tastes, aromas and colors were soon in great demand everywhere, quite often to cover up poor or slightly rotten meat. Even now some Europeans make a curry with leftovers. We can all aspire to season food with Indian finesse. The meats and vegetables in an Indian curry are always of high quality and, like the spice blend itself, are *freshly prepared*.

Neighboring Burma and Ceylon are lands of curries too, as well as rice, fruits, vegetables and coconut. Ceylon's culture dates back to 600 B.C. when the Sinhalese Buddhists arrived from north India. The Hindu Tamils migrated from southern India in two waves separated by several hundred years, so there are, in effect, three cultures, each with its own food preferences. Cool curries with hot spices are popular, fish curry usually being the most fiery. Cinnamon is especially popular.

In preparing the exotic dishes which follow we think that by keeping the seasonings subtle you will ensure greater enjoyment of the now-scrutable secrets of Far Eastern cuisine.

JOOK
Thick Rice Soup

Combine:

**8 dried forest mushrooms*,
   softened and sliced
1 large piece dried
   tangerine peel*
1/2 preserved turnip green*,
   well washed and sliced**
Bring to boil, cover and simmer
while making rice.

Bring to boil:
2-1/2 cups water
Add and cook over high heat,
stirring occasionally:
1 cup unwashed raw rice
Keep a tea kettle of boiling
water ready to add as needed.
After 15 minutes lower heat
slightly. Rice should cook until
it is completely broken up and
gooey, 40 minutes. Add to broth,
cook and stir occasionally, for
1 hour or until broth resembles
a gruel.
Last 15 minutes add:
**3-4 sheets dried sheet bean curd*,
   broken into bite-size pieces
2 cups diced leftover turkey
   meat (or other leftovers)
3 Chinese sausages*,
   sliced on diagonal
boiling water as needed**

Adjust seasoning to taste
with:
**salt and pepper
soy sauce
sesame oil***
Pass bowls of:
**slivered green onions
Chinese parsley* sprigs
small raw fish slices for
   dipping (optional)**
May be made ahead of time.
Serves 8-10

LAW BAK TONG
Turnip Soup

Soften in warm water, drain
and slice:
4 dried forest mushrooms*
Combine:
**2 quarts water
2 pounds beef brisket or stew
   meat cut into 1-1/2-inch cubes
1 teaspoon sugar
2 slices fresh ginger root
1 tablespoon star anise seed*
1 teaspoon fennel seed**
Bring to boil, skim off any
scum that rises to surface and
add:
**softened forest mushrooms
2 pounds Chinese turnips* or
   daikon*, peeled and
   cut into chunks**
Cover and simmer 1-1/2 hours.
Season to taste with salt.
Serves 8

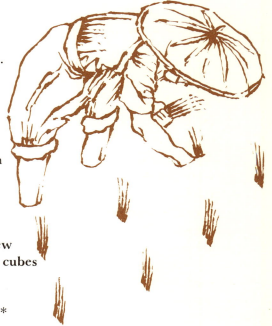

CHINA

STIR FRY VARIATIONS
Beef with Vegetables

Slice diagonally across grain
1/2-inch thick:
skirt or flank steak
For each pound of meat add:
1 tablespoon soy sauce
1/2 teaspoon each salt and sugar
1 teaspoon sherry
1 slice fresh ginger root, minced
1 garlic clove, minced
Heat skillet very hot and add:
1 or 2 tablespoons corn,
  peanut or salad oil, or
  beef suet
When oil begins to sizzle, add
meat. Stir constantly until
redness just starts to disappear,
1 or 2 minutes. Do not overcook.
Immediately remove to dish.
Reheat skillet.
Add:
1 tablespoon oil
a little salt
vegetables
Cook and stir a minute; non-
leafy vegetables will then need
1/3 cup water; leafy vegetables
can cook in the moisture left
from washing. Cover and let steam
2-5 minutes until tender-crisp.
Return meat to skillet, heat and
bind (page 17). Serve immediately
with hot rice.

Suggested vegetables:
broccoli or cauliflower cut
  in 2-inch lengths
asparagus cut on diagonal
  into 1/4-inch lengths
zucchini, summer squash, bitter
  melon, cut in 1/4-inch slices
bok choy**, cabbage, tomatoes,
  bell pepper, onion,
  cut in chunks
string or long beans, snapped
  into 1-1/2-inch lengths

To substitute chicken or pork for
beef, reduce soy by half and do
not remove from pan; cook along
with any of these vegetables.

Add combination of:
fresh pea pods or bean sprouts
canned bamboo shoots, sliced
canned water chestnuts, sliced

For shrimp or other fresh seafood
reduce soy by half and stir fry
as for beef. Do not overcook.
Shrimp should be left whole or
split in half, depending upon
size. Firm white fish should be cut
cut into 1-inch cubes.

**Chinese chard

THI FOON
Bean Thread Noodles

Soak for 10 minutes in warm
water to cover:
8-ounce package bean thread
  noodles*
Drain and cut in half; set aside.
Soak to soften and drain:
2 dozen dried shrimp*
Soak to soften, drain and slice:
7 dried forest mushrooms*
Stir fry (page 17) for
3 minutes in:
1 tablespoon oil
softened shrimp
Add and cook 1 minute:
softened forest mushrooms
Then add and bring to boil:
2 cups water
2 tablespoons soy sauce
Cover and cook over medium
heat 10 minutes, add noodles,
bring back to boil and cook
covered 5-7 minutes to absorb
liquid. The noodles will inflate
3 to 4 times original size.
Season with:
1/4 teaspoon white pepper
1/2 teaspoon sesame oil*
1 teaspoon salt
Add:
1/2 cup chopped green onions
diced cooked ham, chicken
  or pork (optional)
Serves 6

CHOW FAAHN
"Fried" Rice

Make **Egg Garni** (page 16) and
set aside.
Soften in warm water:
4 dried forest mushrooms*
Stir fry (page 17) in:
1 tablespoon corn oil
1-1/2 cups diced ham,
chicken or shrimps
forest mushrooms, thinly sliced
Add:
1 tablespoon soy sauce
1/4 cup water or stock
Bring to boil, lower heat to
simmer, cover and cook 2 minutes.
Combine with:
4 cups hot cooked rice
1/2 teaspoon sesame oil*
1/4 cup chopped green onions
1 tablespoon soy sauce
all but 1/2 cup of egg garni
salt and pepper to taste
Place in serving bowl and garnish
with reserved **egg garni.**
Can be made ahead and heated
in a moderate oven. We prefer
this method as it is not greasy—
it's the soy sauce that "browns"
the rice, not the frying.
Serves 6

HOM DAHN
Salted Chicken or Duck Eggs

Bring to boil then cool:
1-1/2 cups rock salt
1 quart water
Place in large crock or jar with:
1 dozen eggs (chicken or duck)
Cover completely with salt water
and let stand at room temperature
at least 3 weeks. To serve, bring
eggs to boil in fresh water,
simmer 15 minutes, peel and
serve as side dish with any meal.
Yolks will turn a deep orange.

JEN DAHN
Steamed Eggs

See directions for steaming
(page 17). With chopsticks
beat until frothy:
4 eggs
While beating gradually add:
3/4 cup hot (not boiling) water
Add:
1-1/2 tablespoons chopped
green onions
1 teaspoon corn oil
1/8 teaspoon each salt and
sesame oil*
1/2 cup flaked crab, diced
leftover meat, ham, pork
sausage, or Chinese sausage*
Pour into serving dish and steam
20 minutes—**do not let water**
boil. Drizzle oyster sauce*
over and serve immediately.
Serves 6

CHINA

PEA OU HUON DAHN
Peas with Stirred Eggs

Brown in:
1 tablespoon oil
1 Chinese sausage*, diced
   (or 1/2 cup ham)
Add and cook 5 minutes:
1 cup fresh peas
2 tablespoons water
Combine:
4 eggs, beaten
2 tablespoons water
1 tablespoon minced green
   onion and tops
Pour egg mixture over sausage
and peas, let eggs set
slightly, stir and turn
occasionally. Just before
eggs are firm bring edges
to center to form a mound. Flip
over onto heated platter and
serve with rice.
Serves 2-4

CHOW MEIN
Noodle Dish

Soak in warm water to soften,
drain and slice:
6 dried forest mushrooms*
Parboil 3 minutes:
1 recipe Chinese Noodles
   (page 12)
Drain, rinse in cold water and
drain again.
In heavy skillet heat:
2 tablespoons corn oil
Sprinkle with:
1/4 teaspoon salt
Add half the noodles, brown
both sides, turning once;
remove to heated platter and
keep warm. Repeat with rest
of noodles, adding oil and salt
as needed. Remove to platter.

Brown in:
1 tablespoon oil
1 raw chicken breast, sliced
   (or 1/2 pound beef or pork)
Add:
forest mushrooms
1/2 cup each sliced bamboo
   shoots and celery
1/2 cup Chinese chives* or
   green onions,
   cut in 1-inch pieces
2 cups bean sprouts
Cook and stir over medium
heat 1 minute.
Add:
1 teaspoon each soy sauce
   and salt
1/8 teaspoon sugar
1/4 cup water
Cover and cook 5 minutes.
Pour over reserved noodles
and mix in:
1/2 teaspoon sesame oil*
Serves 4-6

GEE GIAK THUEN
Pickled Pigs' Feet

Blanch (page 17) 5 minutes:
3 pounds pigs' feet, split down
center and cut into
2-inch pieces
Drain, rinse and combine with:
3 cups water
3/4 cup vinegar
3/4 - 1 cup brown sugar
2 teaspoons salt
2 tablespoons sliced
fresh ginger root
Bring to boil, cover and simmer
1 hour or until feet are tender.
Serve in bowls with some of
the broth. Rich, gelatinous
and nutritious.
May be made ahead of time.
Serves 6

HEM THUEN JOW GAI YIT
Fried Chicken Wings with
Sweet and Sour Sauce

Remove tips (reserve for soup)
from:
2 pounds chicken wings, cut
at joints
Marinate 1 hour in mixture of:
2 tablespoons soy sauce
1 tablespoon sherry
2 slices fresh ginger root,
minced
2 green onions, chopped
1/2 teaspoon minced garlic
Place wings in bowl with:
1 egg, beaten
Stir to coat well; add and
coat with:

1/2 cup flour
Fry in hot oil, 1/2-inch deep,
one layer at a time, until
golden on both sides. Drain and
place on shredded lettuce.

Combine:
1 cup cold water
2 tablespoons each catsup,
vinegar, cornstarch and sugar
1-1/2 tablespoons plum sauce*
(optional)
Heat until slightly thickened
and adjust seasonings to taste.
Pour over chicken wings and
sprinkle with:
1/4 cup toasted sesame seeds
Serve hot or cold with
preserved mixed vegetable
relish*.
Serves 6

CHINA

SIEW OP
Roast Duck

To prepare marinade, combine,
bring to boil and cool:
1/2 cup soy sauce
1/4 cup sherry
2 tablespoons sugar
2 slices fresh ginger root
1 piece dried tangerine peel*
1/2 teaspoon "5" spice powder*
Marinate, turning several
times, at least 4 hours or
overnight:
1 large Long Island duckling
Into cavity of duck put:
2 stalks green onions
Place on rack and roast, basting
occasionally, in a 375° oven
1 hour. Turn frequently.
Serves 6

GIANG LAT DAYW
Bell Peppers Stuffed with
Shrimp and Pork

Combine for filling:
1/2 pound each ground lean
    pork and minced raw shrimp
1 green onion, finely minced
2 tablespoons cornstarch
1 tablespoon water
2 teaspoons soy sauce
1/2 teaspoon salt
Cut into quarters lengthwise
and then in half again
crosswise:
3 large bell peppers

Remove seeds. Each pepper will
give 8 pieces. Fill each piece
with 1-1/2 tablespoons
filling, pressing well to
hold.
Brown meat side down to a
golden crust in:
2 tablespoons oil
Mash together:
1 garlic clove, minced
1 tablespoon dow see*
1 slice fresh ginger root,
    minced
Add:
1/2 cup water
Turn peppers meat side up, add
above sauce, cover and let
simmer 15 minutes. Carefully
lift each pepper onto heated
serving dish, bind (page 17)
if desired and pour sauce over.
Serves 6

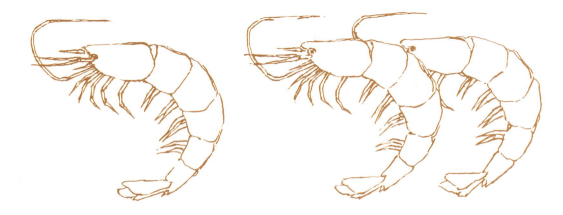

JEN GEE YOOK FOA HUEY
Steamed Pork and Ham

See directions for steaming,
(page 17).
Set in warm water to soften
and then slice:
4 dried forest mushrooms*
Combine:
1 pound lean pork butt, ground
1 tablespoon soy sauce
1-1/2 tablespoons cornstarch
2 tablespoons water
1/2 teaspoon salt
Place in shallow bowl; spread
mixture out evenly, leaving
a slight indentation in center.
Arrange attractively on top:
1/4 pound ham, cut in julienne*
forest mushrooms
Sprinkle with:
1/8 teaspoon sesame oil*
Steam 30 minutes.
Serves 4-6

FAN KIAK GA LEE
JOW GUEY
Tomato-Curry
Whole Fried Fish

Sprinkle generously with salt:
1 whole fish (rock cod,
    perch, etc.), 2 or 3 pounds
Let stand at least 1 hour,
wipe off salt with paper towel

and dry. Over medium heat,
turning once, brown fish in:
1/4 cup hot oil
If fish is thick continue
cooking 10 to 15 minutes longer
in a 350° oven. Sprinkle to taste
with:
salt and pepper

Sauce
Stir fry (page 17) 2 minutes in:
2 tablespoons oil
1 slice fresh ginger root
1 garlic clove
1/2 bell pepper or 1 sweet
    chili pepper, cut up
Add:
3 tomatoes, quartered
1 teaspoon curry powder or
    to taste
Cover and cook until green
pepper is just tender crisp. Bind
(page 17) and pour over fish. If
desired sprinkle with:
sesame oil*
Garnish with:
pickled red ginger*, slivered
Chinese parsley*
Serves 8-10

GUEY BIANG
Fish Cakes

Soften in warm water and mince:
1/4 teaspoon dried tangerine
    peel*
Combine and mix well:
1 pound any firm raw white fish,
    ground
1/2 cup minced canned .
    water chestnuts
2 tablespoons chopped
    green onions
1 tablespoon chopped
    Chinese parsley*
softened tangerine peel
1 tablespoon each soy sauce and
    sherry
2 tablespoons cornstarch
1/2 teaspoon salt
1/4 teaspoon black pepper
Beat together and add to
fish mixture:
4 eggs
2 tablespoons water
Drop by spoonfuls onto hot oiled
skillet to form 3-inch cakes. Let
set and over medium heat brown
lightly; turn to brown other
side, adding more oil as needed.
Do not overcook. If making ahead
undercook slightly and reheat in
a moderate oven.
Makes 18 cakes; serves 6

CHINA

JEN GUEY
Steamed Fish

See directions for steaming
(page 17).
Wash and dry:
1 slice rock cod, sea bass or
  other firm fish, 2-inches thick
Place in shallow bowl and
drizzle over:
1 tablespoon soy sauce
Sprinkle with:
1/4 teaspoon salt
2 slices fresh ginger root,
  slivered
1 green onion, slivered
1/4 teaspoon sesame oil*
Drizzle over all:
1 tablespoon corn oil
Steam 10-15 minutes depending
upon thickness of fish.
Serves 2-4

LAW PAK GO
Turnip Pudding

Soak for 10 minutes in warm
water to soften:
2 tablespoons dried shrimp*
In boiling salted water
cook 10 minutes:
1 pound Chinese turnips*,
  peeled and thinly sliced
Drain and while still hot
mash with:
2 cups rice flour*
3/4 cup cold water
1/4 cup corn oil
1/2 teaspoon salt
Sauté in:
1 tablespoon corn oil
1/4 pound lean pork butt, ground
softened dried shrimp

1 teaspoon soy sauce
Combine with turnip mixture,
pour into oiled 9-inch Pyrex
dish, cover with wax paper and
steam (page 17) 1-1/2 hours
or until center is set.
Immediately sprinkle with:
2 tablespoons each chopped
  green onions and
  Chinese parsley*
1 tablespoon toasted sesame
  seeds
Serve warm or at room
temperature. Or when cool, cut
into squares and brown on both
sides in oil. These are eaten
with brunch or lunch with tea.
Serves 6

MA PWA DOW FU
Pork with Bean Curd

Combine:
1/2 pound lean pork butt, ground
1/2 teaspoon salt
1 teaspoon cornstarch
2 teaspoons each oil and sherry
Brown over medium heat until
pork loses pink color.
Add and sauté 3 minutes:
2 green onions, chopped
1/2 teaspoon each minced fresh
  ginger root and garlic
Add and simmer 10 minutes:
1 12-ounce package firm bean
  curd*, cut in 1/2-inch cubes
1 tablespoon soy sauce
1/2 teaspoon each salt and sugar
1 or 2 red chili peppers (page 17),
  minced
1/4 cup stock
Sprinkle with:
1/2 teaspoon sesame oil*
Serve with boiled rice (page 14).
Serves 4
Note: as in all homestyle cooking,
there are no definite proportions.
Cook according to taste and what
you have on hand. Substitute
beef for the pork, add oyster
sauce* or omit the hot seasoning.
May be made ahead of time.

KIEW THUEY
Wonton Cookies

Work with 2 **wonton skins**
(page 12) at a time. Put one on
top of the other and cut in half.
Make a 1-inch slit lengthwise in
center of each half and pull one
end up and through the slit to
make a loose bow. Continue with
rest of skins. Deep fry a few at
a time until golden, drain on
paper toweling and sprinkle with:
powdered sugar and cinnamon

OW FOO FAH
Almond Float Dessert

Soften in:
1 cup cold water
3 tablespoons plain gelatin
Combine with:
1/3 cup sugar
Dissolve in double boiler,
remove from heat and gradually
add:
3 cups milk
1 tablespoon almond extract
Pour into bowl or mold and
chill until set. Serve
surrounded by chilled fresh
fruits and berries, or chilled
canned mandarin oranges,
kumquats, longans and/or
loquats and some of their syrups.
Serves 6

JAPAN

NUTA (SU MISO AE NUTA AONEGI)
Green Onion Relish with Fish

Cut in 2-inch lengths and blanch (page 17) 30 seconds:
2 bunches green onions
Combine with:
2 tablespoons shirumiso*
1/2 cup rice vinegar*
1 tablespoon sugar
1/2 cup slivered cooked squid, bay shrimp, minced clams or other seafood

OKAZU
Fresh Relishes

Blanch (page 17) 30 seconds vegetables such as:
watercress, spinach, matsuba *, and/or
Blanch 1 minute vegetables such as:
beans, cut in julienne*
Drain, rinse in cold water, drain and press out excess liquid. Serve with dressing of choice:

Combine:
2 tablespoons soy sauce
1 teaspoon sugar
1 tablespoon sesame seeds

Combine:
2 tablespoons each shirumiso* rice vinegar* and sugar

Combine and cook, stirring constantly, until smooth and thickened:
1 egg yolk, beaten
2 tablespoons rice vinegar*
1 tablespoon each sugar and sake*
1/2 teaspoon salt
1/4 teaspoon soy sauce
Cool before dressing vegetables.

Dressings may also be used on raw vegetables such as cucumbers, grated daikon* or white turnips, often seasoned with a little grated fresh ginger root.

TAKARA MUSHI
Steamed Pumpkin Soup

Select:
a well-shaped pumpkin
that will fit into your steaming pot. Cut off the top and reserve. Remove seeds and pulp from cavity and fill with a mixture of:
2 cups chicken broth
2 tablespoons each shirumiso* and sherry
2 teaspoons sugar
4 dried forest mushrooms*, softened and sliced
1/2 teaspoon salt
1/4 teaspoon pepper
(For a larger pumpkin, increase proportionately.)
Replace lid and for easy removal from pot wrap in cheesecloth. Place on a dish in the pot, fill with enough boiling water to cover the dish, cover pot and steam 35 minutes.
Then add:
1 cup fresh peas
2 cups raw shrimp
Cover and steam 10 more minutes or until pumpkin flesh is tender. Beautiful and spectacular.
Serves 6 or more

DASHI
Basic Broth

Break into several pieces:
1 6x2-inch piece kombu*
Combine with:
6 cups water
1-1/2 cups katsuobushi*
1/2 teaspoon salt
1/8 teaspoon sugar
Bring to boil and cook rapidly
3 minutes. Strain. Repeat,
cooking 5 minutes, if stronger
dashi is desired.

MISOSHIRU
Miso Soup

Strain into:
3 cups boiling strong Dashi
1/3 cup shirumiso*
Adjust to taste with:
more miso, soy sauce and salt
Serve with garnish of:
lemon peel
minced chives
Pass aji oil*. This healthful
dish is often served for
breakfast.

SHIGI YAKI
Roasted Eggplant

Turning often until centers are
soft, roast directly over
hot coals:
Japanese eggplants
When done, slit skin to partially
open and fill with:
grated fresh ginger root
soy sauce

MUSHI IMO
Steamed Sweet Potatoes

Steam until soft:
sweet potatoes
Peel and sprinkle with:
salt to taste
This is a favorite afternoon
treat for school children.

NINGIN SHIRAE
Carrot Salad

Cook until carrots are just
tender-crisp:
4 cups julienned* carrots
1/2 cup water
1-1/2 tablespoons sugar
2 tablespoons soy sauce
Cool and add:
1 cup diced bean curd*
1/4 cup shirumiso*
May be made ahead of time.
Serves 6

TERIYAKI
Marinade for Barbecuing

Combine:
1/2 cup each soy sauce and sake*
1/3 cup sugar
This marinade may be used for
many different kinds of meat.
Cut-up chicken should be
marinated 3-4 hours, chuck roast
overnight. Use it to baste while
cooking firm white fish cut
into slices and skewered.

JAPAN

TAMAGO UDON
Noodles with Egg

Cook in:
Dashi (page 33)
udon*
Beat slightly:
1 egg per person
In small pan add to:
1/4 cup boiling water
Cover until set and place on
top of udon and dashi.
Sprinkle with:
slivered green onions

SUSHI
Cold Rice

Turn into wooden bowl (wood
absorbs excess moisture):
6 cups cooked pearl rice
   (page 14)
Dress with mixture of:
1/3 cup rice vinegar*
2 tablespoons sugar
2 teaspoons salt
toasted sesame seeds (optional)
Cool and form oval shape on
serving platter. Garnish with
any combination of:
barely cooked green peas or beans
carrots cut in julienne*
pickled red ginger *
   cut in julienne
dried forest mushrooms *
   softened, sliced and cooked
Egg Garni (page 16)
baby shrimp or other seafood
cooked chicken cut in julienne
dried baby fish soaked in equal
   parts vinegar and water,
   rinsed and dried
nori*
May be made ahead of time.

MISO YAKI
Broiled Miso Fish

Combine:
1 tablespoon each sake *
   and sugar
1/2 cup shirumiso*
Cover with miso mixture and
refrigerate 24 hours:
2 pounds halibut, sea bass or
   salmon steaks
Scrape off as much miso mixture
as possible and broil fish
5-8 minutes per side. Do not
overcook. Serve with:
grated daikon*
sprinkling of soy sauce
Serves 4

NIKU NO MISO YAKI
Miso Beef

Combine:
1/4 cup akamiso*
2 tablespoons soy sauce
1-1/2 tablespoons sugar
**1 slice fresh ginger root,
    minced**
1 green onion and tops, chopped
Slice thinly on diagonal and
marinate in above mixture
10 minutes:
1 pound flank steak
Quickly sauté meat in:
**2 tablespoons finely minced
    beef suet**
Serve with rice.
Serves 4-6

SASHIMI
Raw Fish

Cut into thin slices:
**very fresh fish (such as striped
    bass, spearfish, tuna, porgy,
    red snapper, sea bass or
    other lean fish; crab,
    shrimp, abalone or squid)**
Arrange slices attractively
on bed of:
shredded lettuce and/or daikon*
Garnish with:
cucumber slivers
shredded raw carrot
shingiku*
matsuba*
Mix and place in small dish
on side of plate:
**equal amounts of water
    and wasabi***

For dipping sauce, mix to taste:
**1/2 cup each Dashi (page 33)
    and Mirin* or rice vinegar***
salt
grated fresh ginger root

NIZAKANA
Boiled Fish

Bring to boil:
**1/4 cup each sake * soy sauce
    and water**
2 teaspoons sugar
Add:
**1 whole fish head, from bass,
    rock cod or snapper (fish head
    contains the best and sweetest
    flesh) or**
1 2-pound thick piece of fish
Cook slowly, basting constantly,
10-15 minutes until fish is just
cooked and sauce begins to
thicken. There will be hardly
any sauce left. Garnish with:
slivered green onions
Serve with rice.

JAPAN

KANTEN AZUKI
Agar-Agar with Sweet Red Bean Sauce (Gelatin Dessert)

Combine:
3 cups water
1/2 cup sugar
Soak 5 minutes in this mixture:
1 stick kanten*, cut up
Bring just to boil and simmer 10 minutes. Add:
1 teaspoon almond extract
Pour into shallow dish, cool and refrigerate until set. When ready to serve, cut into 1-inch cubes and place in individual serving bowls. Cover each serving with:
2 tablespoons chilled sweet azuki*

HIYASHI SOBA
Buckwheat Noodles Over Ice

Drop into boiling salted water:
1 12-ounce package soba*
Bring back to boil, drain, rinse in cold water and drain. Place on bed of ice and top with:
1/4 cup chopped green onion
toasted nori* to taste
Serve with small dish of dip.

For dip, bring to boil and cool:
1/2 cup each Dashi (page 33) and soy sauce
2 tablespoons sake *
1 tablespoon sugar
Serves 4-6

UDON KITSUNE
Noodles with Fried Bean Curd

Cook in:
Dashi (page 33)
udon*
Top with:
fried bean curd*, cut up
slivered green onions
drizzle of aji oil*

YAKKO TOFU
Bean Curd on Ice

Dice and place in bowl of ice:
very fresh smooth bean curd*
Top to taste with:
soy sauce
dried bonito flakes* (optional)
This is a good hot weather dish.

GREEN TEA ICE CREAM

Blend together:
1 pint softened vanilla ice cream
1 tablespoon green tea powder*
Return to freezer until ready to serve. Serve with a topping of sweet azuki*.

KOOK MU
Turnip Soup

Combine:
1/2 pound flank steak, sliced
    diagonally 1/8-inch thick
1/2 cup green onions, cut in
    julienne*
1/2 pound turnips, preferably
    Chinese*, cut in 1/2-inch
    squares
1 tablespoon soy sauce
1 teaspoon salt
1/4 teaspoon each pepper and
    sesame oil*
1/4 cup water
Stir fry (page 17) in:
1 tablespoon oil
Cook only until meat begins to
lose its redness.
Add:
1 quart water
Bring just to boil and
simmer 15 minutes.
Serves 4-6

KOOK DAEHAP SIGUMCHI
Clam and Spinach Soup

Combine:
1/2 pound ground lean beef
1 slice fresh ginger root,
    minced
1 garlic clove, minced
Stir fry (page 17) in:
1 tablespoon oil
Add and simmer, covered,
20 minutes:
4 cups boiling beef stock
Add:
2 cups cut-up fresh spinach
1 pound soft bean curd*, cubed
30 small mussels or clams,
    well scrubbed
    (or 1 10-ounce can baby clams)
Over medium heat
bring back to boil.
Remove from heat and add:
1/2 teaspoon sesame oil*
Serves 4-6

KOOK SOO
Cold Noodle Soup

Skim fat from:
chilled non-gelatinous
    clear broth
Mix with:
cold cooked fresh noodles
    (page 12)
Add:
juice to taste from Kim Chee
    (following recipe)
Serve for a cool lunch, adding ice
cubes to each bowl if desired.

KOREA

KIM CHEE

A relish served with almost every Korean dish and used in cooking as well. Make large amounts to keep on hand to make the effort worthwhile.

Choose firm, white heads of:
**Chinese cabbage (about
    4-1/2 pounds)**
Cut into 1-1/2-inch lengths and sprinkle with:
1/3 cup salt
Let stand at least 4 hours until cabbage is wilted.
Drain off excess water and combine with:
**2 tablespoons each minced fresh
    ginger root and minced garlic**
1/2 cup chopped green onion
**1 or 2 small red hot chili
    peppers (page 17), minced**
1 teaspoon paprika

Fill clean glass jars with relish up to 2 inches from top, add cold water to top of relish and cover, but do not seal. Let sit at room temperature 2 or 3 days until fermentation begins. The second day check for saltiness, adding more if needed. Bubbles will rise to top when relish is fermented enough. Tighten lids and refrigerate indefinitely.
Makes about 3 quarts

BAB KIM CHEE
Pork and Rice with Kim Chee

Combine:
6 cups cooked rice
2 cups cooked shredded pork
1 cup Kim Chee, chopped
1/4 cup chopped green onions
1 garlic clove, minced
Serve heated, or at room temperature.
May be made ahead of time.
Serves 6

OYI NAMUL KOGI
Cucumber Salad with Beef

Sprinkle with salt:
3 young cucumbers, sliced
Let stand 20 minutes and pat dry.
Marinate in:
1 tablespoon soy
1 teaspoon sugar
1/2 tablespoon sesame oil*
1 garlic clove, minced
1 slice fresh ginger root, minced
1/2 pound thinly sliced beef
Stir fry (page 17) in:
1 tablespoon oil
Toss with:
cucumbers
Serve hot or cold.
May be made ahead of time.
Serves 4

HOBAHK JUHN
Zucchini-Beef Omelets

Combine:
1 pound zucchini, cut
    into julienne*
1/2 teaspoon salt
1/4 teaspoon pepper
4 tablespoons flour
6 eggs, beaten
1/2 pound lean ground beef
1/2 teaspoon sesame oil*
Heat:
1 tablespoon oil
Drop batter by spoonfuls into
hot oil; after egg has set
slightly scrape runny edges up
and around to make a 3-inch
omelet. Fry on both sides
until golden, adding more oil
as needed. Keep warm until all
omelets are fried. Serve with
rice and Cho Jung.
Serves 4

TU BU
Bean Curd

Cut into 1/4-inch slices:
firm bean curd*
Stir fry (page 17) and dip in
Cho Jung sauce to serve.

CHO JUNG
Sauce for Dipping

Combine:
1/4 cup soy sauce
1 tablespoon vinegar
1 teaspoon sugar
1/4 teaspoon sesame oil*
1 tablespoon finely chopped
    green onions
1/2 teaspoon pounded toasted
    sesame seeds

TOASTED LAVER
Toasted Seaweed Sheets

Combine:
1 tablespoon each corn oil
    and sesame oil*
With fingers rub onto one side
only of:
10 to 12 sheets nori*
Layer sheets until all are
oiled. Always place the oiled
sheet on the bottom of the
stack. Roll up and cover with
wax paper; let stand 15
minutes. Heat an iron skillet
until very hot but not smoking.
With fingers holding the 2
ends of a sheet, toast for 1
second, lift, turn and toast
until entire surface of sheet
is toasted. Sprinkle lightly
with salt, repeat with rest of
layers, stack, cut into
quarters and serve with hot rice.
May be made ahead of time.

KOREA

KALBI KUI
Barbecued Short Ribs

Combine:
3 garlic cloves, minced
2 green onions and tops,
    chopped
1/2 cup soy sauce
1 teaspoon sesame oil*
1 teaspoon toasted sesame seeds
1 tablespoon each sugar and
    vinegar
2 tablespoons fresh ginger
    root, minced
1/2 teaspoon black pepper
Pour over:
4 pounds meaty beef short ribs
    which have been scored by
    cutting every half-inch almost
    to the bone in a crisscross
    pattern
Marinate, turning frequently,
3 hours or overnight. Cook over
hot coals, turning often to
avoid burning, 15-20 minutes.
Serves 6

TAHK KUI
Barbecued Chicken

Follow above directions,
substituting 2 fryers, cut up,
for the ribs. Serve with Salad.

Salad
Blanch (page 17) 1 minute:
1 bunch watercress, large stems
    removed and then cut up, or
    1 pound bean sprouts (or
    combination)
Drain; combine with:
1 tablespoon soy sauce
1/2 teaspoon sesame oil*
1 tablespoon lemon juice
    or vinegar
1 teaspoon sugar
2 tablespoons each chopped
    onions and toasted
    sesame seeds
Chill well before serving.

LETTHOH
Noodle-Rice Table

Sauté until golden in:
3 tablespoons peanut oil
1 cup raw rice, washed and
    drained
1/4 teaspoon cayenne pepper
Add and mix well:
2 cups water
Bring to gentle boil, cover and
cook over medium low heat
20 minutes or until rice is dry
and tender. Set aside.

Soak in warm water to soften,
drain and set aside:
4 ounces transparent noodles
    (bean thread noodles*)
4 ounces rice noodles (py
    mei fun*)
Heat in pan:
3 tablespoons peanut oil
Brown separately and set aside:
2 cups thinly sliced onions
    and 1/8 teaspoon saffron
6-8 garlic cloves, minced
Cook in boiling salted water 2 to
4 minutes separately:
the softened transparent noodles
the rice noodles
4 ounces egg noodles
Drain and set aside.

Prepare and place in separate
dishes:
1 pound bean sprouts, blanched
    (page 17) 30 seconds and
    drained
2 cups shredded carrots
2 cups shredded cucumber
2 cups grated green papaya
    (substitute finely shredded
    green cabbage)
4 hard-cooked eggs, quartered
16 small potatoes, boiled
1 4-ounce package shrimp chips*,
    deep fried and crumbled
1/4 cup lemon juice
1/2 cup gram powder (substitute
    farina, toasted in dry pan
    5 minutes)
1/2 cup chili flakes (substitute
    dried hot red peppers,
    crushed)
Patis*
prepared onions and garlic

To serve, arrange rice and
noodles on large platter (room
temperature) and have guests help
themselves to portions. Desired
vegetables are then placed
on top, then 2 egg quarters,
2 potatoes and remaining
ingredients to taste. Bowls of
hot hingyo (any clear vegetable
or mushroom broth) are served
as an accompaniment.
Serves 8

HIN THEE HINGYO
Vegetable Curry

Sauté until transparent in:
3 tablespoons peanut oil
2 onions, thinly sliced
2 garlic cloves, minced
Add, stir and cook 5 minutes:
1 tablespoon each cracked
    coriander and poppy seed
1/2 tablespoon cumin seed
1/4 teaspoon cayenne pepper
pinch saffron
2 teaspoons turmeric powder
1/2 teaspoon each fenugreek
    and mustard seed
1 teaspoon salt
Add and mix well:
2 cups hot chicken broth
Add, cover and cook 5-8
minutes:
2 cups raw diced potatoes
1 small head cauliflower
    broken into flowerets
Add and cook 5 minutes:
2 cups shredded Chinese cabbage
    (or iceberg lettuce)
1/2 pound Japanese eggplant,
    unpeeled and cut into
    1-1/2-inch chunks
1/2 pound okra
Serve immediately with plain
boiled rice.
Serves 4

BURMA/CEYLON

POACHED SALMON

Boil together:

1 quart water
1 teaspoon Patis*
1 slice fresh ginger root
2 green onions, chopped
Add:
whole salmon
Poach 10 minutes per pound.
Serve on boiled rice noodles (py
mei fun*) which have been
moistened with a little poaching
water.
This is a favorite meal in Burma.

VATA CAPPAN
Coconut Custard

Combine:

4 eggs, well beaten
3 tablespoons sugar
1/4 teaspoon each salt and nutmeg
2 cups milk, scalded and
     cooled to lukewarm
1 cup shredded coconut* (omit
     sugar if using sweetened brand)*
Pour into greased or oiled
1-1/2-quart baking dish or
6 individual custard cups. Bake
in a 350° oven 25 to
30 minutes (15 minutes for cups)
or until custard tests done.
Serve hot or cold.
Serves 6

GREEN CHUTNEY

Place in blender:
2 cups fresh coriander* stems
    and leaves, cut up
1-4 hot green chilis (page 17)
2 garlic cloves
1 tablespoon fresh ginger
    root, minced
1 onion, cut up
1/2 cup shredded dried coconut*
1 teaspoon sugar
1/2 teaspoon salt
1/4 cup lemon juice
1/2 cup water
Purée just long enough to make
a smooth paste. Serve as
accompaniment to any curry.
Good on Nan (page 6) with
cottage cheese.
Makes 2 cups

EGG CURRY

Sauté until onions start to
brown in:
2 tablespoons oil or butter
2 onions, thinly sliced
1 teaspoon finely minced
    fresh ginger root
1 garlic clove, finely minced
1-2 dried hot red chili
    peppers (page 17), crushed
1/2 teaspoon each turmeric
    powder and salt
Lower heat and add:
1 cup coconut milk (page 17)
Cover and simmer 20 minutes.
Then add:
8 hard-cooked eggs, halved
Simmer 5 minutes to heat eggs.
Sprinkle with:
fresh chopped coriander*
Serve with Dal (following recipe)
or plain rice.
If desired, when adding coconut
milk add and cook until tender
to total about 1-1/2 cups:
okra
cauliflowerets
diced eggplant
sliced potatoes
string beans, cut up
broccoli flowerets
or any combination.
In India a side dish of yoghurt,
mint and garlic is always
served with curries.
Serves 4

DAL

Combine:
1 cup yellow mung dal*
2 cups water
1/2 teaspoon salt
Bring to boil, lower heat
slightly, cook until moisture
has evaporated, lower heat
to lowest, cover and simmer
20 minutes.
Sauté until golden in:
3 tablespoons butter
1 large onion, diced
1 garlic clove, minced
2 tablespoons chopped fresh
    coriander* (optional)
1/8 teaspoon cayenne pepper
Toss in the cooked dal
and mix well.
Serves 4-6

INDIA

ROGAN JOSH
Lamb Curry

For marinade purée in blender:
3 **garlic cloves**
1 **tablespoon-grated fresh**
   ginger root
2 **whole cloves**
1 **2-inch cinnamon stick**
3 **peeled cardamom pods, cracked**
1/4 **cup fresh coriander***
   leaves and stems
1/2 **teaspoon turmeric**
2-4 **hot chili peppers (page 17)**
1/2 **teaspoon salt**
3/4 **cup water**

Marinate at least 2 hours in
above mixture:
2 **pounds boneless lamb cubes or**
3 **pounds lamb shoulder stew**
Sauté until golden in:
6 **tablespoons butter**
4 **large onions, thinly sliced**
Add marinade and meat;
simmer gently 1 hour or until
lamb is tender.
Serve with Dal (page 43) or rice.
May be made ahead of time.
Serves 4-6

SEMIYA
Vermicelli Dessert

Brown, stirring and turning
constantly over medium heat in:
2 **tablespoons butter**
2 **ounces imported**
   Indian vermicelli**
Add:
1 **cup evaporated milk**
1/4 **teaspoon powdered cardamom**
Cook, stirring occasionally,
until moisture is evaporated and
mixture is thick and creamy.
Add and stir to dissolve:
1 **tablespoon jaggary***
Mound in a bowl and drizzle over:
1 **tablespoon rose water**
Sprinkle with:
3 **tablespoons slivered,**
   toasted blanched almonds
Serves 6
**Extra thin vermicelli sold in
East Indian stores. Fine wheat
vermicelli may be substituted.

RAITHA
Yoghurt and Vegetable Salad

Combine:
1 cup yoghurt
3-4 cups mixed vegetables such
    as raw spinach and
    cucumber, cooked
    potatoes or eggplant
1/2 cup chopped onions
1 dried red chili pepper,
    crushed or 1/8 teaspoon
    cayenne pepper
2 tablespoons minced fresh mint
    leaves
1/2 teaspoon each cumin powder
    and salt
1/4 teaspoon black pepper
Can also season cut-up tomatoes,
minced onions and yoghurt with
curry to taste.
Serves 4-6

TIKKAS
Barbecued Chicken

Marinate at least 4 hours in:
1 cup yoghurt
1 garlic clove, minced
1 onion, minced
1/2 teaspoon each cinnamon,
    cumin powder and
    black pepper
2 peeled cardamom pods,
    cracked
1/4 teaspoon each powdered
    ginger, powdered cloves,
    nutmeg and cayenne pepper
1 teaspoon salt
2 pounds chicken, cut into
    small pieces
Skewer chicken and broil over
hot coals, turning frequently,
5-7 minutes per side. Baste with
marinade. Chicken should be
crisp.
Serve with dip made by
combining:
1 cup yoghurt
1 garlic clove, minced
1/2 cup fresh chopped mint
Good with Nan (page 6).
Serves 6

CARROT HALWA
Carrot Dessert

Grate in blender:
1-1/2 pounds carrots
2 cups milk
Cook 1-1/2 hours or until all
moisture has evaporated. Then
add:
1/4 cup butter
3/4 cup jaggary*
2 peeled cardamom pods,
    cracked
Mix well and cook 10 minutes.
Mixture should be dry. Serve hot
or cold. Just before serving
drizzle over:
1 tablespoon rose water
Garnish with:
slivered, toasted, blanched
    almonds
May be made ahead of time.
Serves 6-8

MIDDLE EAST

ALTHOUGH Dalmatian ants are said to chew grain into dough, shape the dough into patties and bake the patties in the sun, bread making is usually considered to be a hallmark of civilized man. Americans tend to think of the light, fluffy white loaf in a gaily colored, moisture-proof wrapper as a highly civilized food indeed, for the Western World has generally adopted the "fermented garden of bacteria of yesterday's dough" that so astonished a careless ancient Egyptian cook and resulted in leavened bread. The loaf of bread that, along with a book of verse, a jug of wine and a true love, turned Omar Khayyam's wilderness into Paradise was probably flat, as much of the bread in the Middle East is today.

Omar's loaf and the ubiquitous roasted lamb symbolize what occurred in the Middle East about 9,000 years ago. It was in Kurdistan, many believe, in the New Stone Age, that man turned from a nomadic hunter into herdsman, from food gatherer into crop planter. Wild sheep were domesticated for butchering; wild grasses and legumes were cultivated for harvesting. The consequent need for recording property rights and trade transactions led to written language and mathematics; transportation and communication spread knowledge east and west, and the Middle East became the funnel between the two.

Soon Middle Easterners were living on far more than bread and lamb alone. Rice supplemented wheat and barley; sugarcane from India became a sweetener even more widely used than honey; olives, pomegranates, figs, dates, almonds, lemons and citrons brought from Asia were spread around the Mediterranean by Moslem colonists. Surprisingly, many ancient dishes other than bread still exist in very early forms; *fava*, for example, with its thick stew of dried peas, lentils or chickpeas, olive oil, parsley, oregano, onion and garlic. *Bulghur*, boiled wheat (then dried), probably the forerunner of bread, is still extensively used in soups and stuffings or as a substitute for rice in pilaf. It's also pounded with finely ground lamb to make *kibbeh*, "the hamburger of the Eastern Mediterranean." Then, of course, there are the precious spices, as widely savored as in India, though used somewhat more sparingly.

Middle East foods could be categorized by nationality and religious faith, but it's more fascinating to observe the patina of layer upon layer of long-dead civilizations in today's peasant foods. Food factories haven't yet replaced primitive inverted iron "ovens" for baking *shrak*, Bedouin whole-wheat crusts that, together with rice, boiled lamb and seasoned butter or *ghee*, make up the main dish for a formal tent dinner, the *mansaf*. Bread is still largely homemade or bought daily fresh and warm. Dates and other simple fruits are mainstays of many diets as they have been for centuries. Iraqi *masgoof*, outdoor broiled fish from the Tigris and Euphrates, is probably as old as civilization itself. Everyone seems to like the Israeli "hot dog," *felafel*, an old deep-fried delight of chickpeas ground with bulghur and spices. In addition to the East Indian spices, *mahlah* from black cherry kernels, *sumak*, sour *verjuice* squeezed from unripe grapes as of old, and dried whole limes add unfamiliar distinctive flavors.

The milk (soured fast to keep) and sword-meat (kebabs) cherished by Turks a thousand years ago are now prepared with borrowed, more modern techniques, but the Turkish still lay claim to knowing hundreds of ways of preparing a 1500-year-old import from India, the eggplant. Still, in some primitive regions, nomadic peasants jealously guard their own precious cultures of yoghurt, the food that "fortifies the soul." Tomatoes, green and red peppers, and corn from the New World have been adopted in certain areas, but *yakhui* (olive oil vegetable dishes), *dolma* (ground meat, rice, herbs and spices stuffed into leaves or vegetables) or *chelo kebab* (Iran's "national dish" of rice, marinated lamb, yoghurt, raw egg and *sumak*) depend entirely on traditional foods of much longer standing.

Combinations of fruit and meat are typical of Iran and are also favored in Israel's developing national cuisine. Hebrews from all over the world are eagerly adapting ancestral dishes to indigenous foods in their energetic young nation, but at the same time they're broadening their array of crops with irrigation and experimentation. Exciting new gourmet dishes are sure to result.

Religious restrictions, mostly having to do with meat, forbid the eating of pork to Muslim and Jew alike. Meat and dairy products are recognized as separate food classes, and for the Orthodox Jews special meat-slaughtering methods are prescribed and there is abstinence from seafood without scales or fins. *Pareve*, or neutral foods like vegetables, grains, fruits, breads and pastries with vegetable shortening, along with varied seasonings for lamb, beef, kid and fish (even camel for the Arabs) leave plenty of room in which an ingenious chef can maneuver. Poverty is a harder taskmaster. Peasants like the *Fellameen* in their hovels along the Nile hardly ever see meat at all, fish only occasionally. Their "poor men's meats"—*fool* (boiled seasoned beans) and *tamiya* (deep-fried fava-bean patties with garlic, onions, green coriander, parsley and cayenne)—must not be too bad, however, for they're served in good restaurants. Also, with new irrigation waters for the desert from the Aswan Dam and newly discovered deep underground lakes, the *Fellameen* and others anticipate more raw tomatoes, cucumbers and turnips as well as cooked beans, lentils, zucchini and okra stewed in butter.

One can't overlook other Middle East delicacies like *phyllo* dough, so thin as to be almost transparent, so versatile as to be equally delicious wrapped around spicy ground meat or dripping honey in multi-layered *baklava*; crocks of buttery melted tallow from the huge tails of force-fed sheep; *samneh*, bright yellow sheep or goat milk butter; *feta* (goat milk) cheese; and many other treats too numerous to mention. Let's hope that the Middle East can withstand the onslaught of modernization and petroleum popularity by keeping its glance partially fixed on its diverse cultural inheritance. Otherwise food secrets of older civilizations may be forgotten. ten.

ARABIA

TABOOLEH
Cracked Wheat Salad

Soak 15 minutes:
**1 cup bulghur (fine cracked
wheat), washed in cold water**
Drain well and add:
**3 medium tomatoes, peeled
and chopped**
**1 cucumber, peeled, seeded
and chopped**
1 cup chopped parsley
1/2 cup chopped fresh mint
1 teaspoon chopped fresh oregano
**3 tablespoons chopped green
onions**
**6 tablespoons each olive oil
and lemon juice**
1 teaspoon salt
Mix well and adjust seasonings to
taste. Mound on serving plate and
surround with tender leaves of
Romaine lettuce standing on end.
Serve with Pita (page 7).
May be made ahead of time.
Serves 4-6

BABA GHANNOUJ
Eggplant Dip

In a 400°oven bake 40 minutes
or until soft:
1 large eggplant
Peel and mash with:
5 tablespoons tahini*
1 garlic clove, pressed
3-4 tablespoons lemon juice
1/2 teaspoon salt
Adjust seasonings and lemon
juice to taste. Mound on serving
plate and pour over mound:
2 tablespoons olive oil
Sprinkle with:
3 tablespoons chopped parsley
Serve with Pita (page 7).
Serves 4

JAJIK
Cucumber Salad

Combine:
1 cup yoghurt
2 cucumbers, peeled and chopped
1/4 teaspoon salt
1 garlic clove, pressed
1 teaspoon olive oil
1 tablespoon minced fresh mint
Serves 4

RIZ BI SH´AREH
Rice and Vermicelli

Sauté until golden in:
1/4 cup butter
1/2 cup short vermicelli
Add:
1 cup long grain rice
1/2 teaspoon salt
2 cups hot water
Boil gently 5 minutes, lower
heat, cover and simmer 20 minutes
until rice is tender and water
is absorbed. This is eaten with
almost every meal.
Serves 4

SHOURABIT´ADS
Red Lentil Soup with Lamb

Combine, bring to boil, cover
and simmer 1 hour:
2 cups ads majroosh (red lentils)
1 pound or more lamb shanks
6 cups water
1-1/2 teaspoons salt
1/2 teaspoon black pepper
Sauté until soft in:
3 tablespoons olive oil
1 large onion, chopped
1 garlic clove, minced
Add:
4 cups chopped Swiss chard
Cook and stir until chard is
wilted. Add to soup and simmer
15 minutes. Then add:
1/4 cup lemon juice
Adjust seasonings and serve
with lamb shank on side, or cut
up in the soup.
The red lentils turn a golden
color making the soup attractive
with the green of the chard.
Thick and creamy.
May be made ahead of time.
Serves 6

MILAF MASHIVI
Skewered Liver

Blanch (page 17) 1 minute, cut
into chunks and set aside:
3 onions
3 bell peppers
Combine:
1 garlic clove, finely minced
3 tablespoons minced fresh mint
1 teaspoon salt
2 tablespoons each olive oil
   and lemon juice
1/4 teaspoon black pepper
Slice, cut into 1-1/2-inch
pieces and marinate 1 hour in
above mixture:
1 pound beef or lamb liver
Skewer alternately with:
onion and bell pepper chunks
Brush a little marinade on onion
and pepper and broil 2 to 3
minutes on each side. Do not
overcook.
Serves 4

ISRAEL

FELAFEL
Garbanzo Bean Croquettes

Cook until tender, drain and
mash:
1 cup dry garbanzo beans
Soak 10 minutes in hot water
to cover:
**1/4 cup fine bulghur (cracked)
wheat**
Combine cooked garbanzos and
soaked bulghur with:
2 garlic cloves, finely minced
3 tablespoons bread crumbs
1 egg, beaten
**1/2 teaspoon each cumin powder,
salt and black pepper**
1/4 teaspoon cayenne pepper
**1 teaspoon minced fresh
coriander***
Shape into 12 balls, roll in
flour and fry until golden
in deep fat. Drain on paper
toweling. Cut a pocket in
Pita bread discs (page 7).
Place a croquette in each
and fill with a spoonful
of relish (see below) and
Tahini (see below). Pass olives
and vinegar pickles. May be
made ahead of time and reheated.

Relish
Combine:
1 cucumber, finely minced
2 tomatoes, finely minced
1 bell pepper, finely minced
1/2 cup chopped parsley

TAHINI
Dip

Combine in blender and purée:
1/2 cup tahini*
1/2 teaspoon salt
1 garlic clove, minced
1/8 teaspoon cayenne pepper
1/4 cup lemon juice
**2 tablespoons chopped
fresh coriander***
1 tablespoon olive oil

MUNKACZINA
Orange Salad

Combine and serve on lettuce
leaves:
4 oranges, peeled and thinly
    sliced crosswise
2 medium onions, thinly
    sliced crosswise
1 cup pitted black olives
3 tablespoons each olive oil
    and lemon juice
salt and pepper to taste
Serves 4

SALATASI
Salad

Dress slices of ripe tomatoes
with fresh mint or dill, parsley,
olive oil and lemon juice.
Arrange on platter with shredded
lettuce, radishes, Greek olives,
green onions, grated carrots,
and lemon wedges. Just before
serving drizzle with olive oil
and lemon juice.
Or arrange on shredded lettuce:
cooked vegetables such as
carrots, peas, beans and
artichoke hearts, raw tomatoes
stuffed with rice and green
pepper, and Greek olives.
Sprinkle with olive oil and
chopped parsley and garnish
with lemon wedges.

TARABA
Spinach Leaves with Lamb

Combine:
1 pound ground lean lamb
1/4 cup peeled, chopped, ripe
    tomatoes
1/4 cup chopped parsley
2 teaspoons minced oregano
2/3 cup finely minced onion
1/4 cup finely minced
    green onions
2 teaspoons lemon juice
1 teaspoon salt
1/2 teaspoon black pepper
1/4 teaspoon cayenne pepper

Dip into boiling water for
1 minute and drain:
**large leaves from 2 pounds
    spinach**
Spread leaves out on paper
toweling. Place 2-3 teaspoons
filling on stem end of leaves,
depending upon size. Fold stem
end up and over, then fold in
outer edges and roll. Place
seam side down in heavy
aluminum or Teflon skillet
containing mixture of:

1 cup peeled and chopped
    ripe tomatoes
1 tablespoon lemon juice or
    to taste
1/2 teaspoon salt
1/4 teaspoon black pepper
Cover and cook over medium heat
15-25 minutes, depending on size
of rolls, adding stock and lemon
juice if juices boil away.
Remove cover and let liquid boil
down if too juicy.
Serve with Pilau (page 14).
Makes 48 medium or
24 large rolls

KILIC BALIGI SISDE
Swordfish Kebobs

Marinate 2-4 hours in:
**1/4 cup each lemon juice,
    olive oil and minced onion
1 garlic clove, minced
3 bay leaves, crushed
2 pounds swordfish cut into
    1-inch cubes**
Blanch (page 17) 1 minute
    and drain:
**1-2 bell peppers cut into
    1-inch chunks**
Drain fish and skewer
alternately with peppers.
Sprinkle lightly with salt and
black pepper and, basting with
marinade, broil 3 minutes on
each side over charcoal.
Serves 4

TURKEY

SALONIKA TOTI
Mixed Lamb Kebob

Combine and let stand at least
1 hour:
2 onions, thinly sliced
1/2 cup lemon juice
2 tablespoons olive oil
Cut into 1-inch chunks:
1 pound each lamb liver, hearts
   and trimmed kidneys
Soak 1 hour in:
water to cover
2 tablespoons lemon juice
Drain and wipe dry. Skewer
alternately with:
4 slices bacon, cut in 1-inch
   pieces
1 unpeeled eggplant, cut in
   1-inch chunks
Dip into batter (see Fish and
Chips, page 122) and fry until
crisp in deep fat or oil. Serve
with the marinated onions, fresh
corn on the cob and Orange
Salad (page 53).
Serves 6-8

DOLMAS TOMATES
Stuffed Tomatoes

Sauté until transparent in:
3 tablespoons olive oil
1/2 cup chopped onion
1 garlic clove, minced
Add and sauté until golden:
1/2 cup rice, washed
   and drained
Add and bring to gentle boil:
1 cup water
1/4 teaspoon each allspice
   and black pepper
1/2 teaspoon salt
Cook, uncovered, over medium
heat until water evaporates.
Then add:
2 cups chopped raw zucchini
1 cup chopped fresh spinach
2 tablespoons each chopped
   mint and currants
Cover and simmer 15 minutes.
Cool. Slice off top and remove
pulp from:
8-12 ripe tomatoes
Fill with stuffing and
bake in a 325° oven 20 minutes.
Serves 6-8

DJEDJAD
Chicken Roasted with Apricots

Combine:
1/4 cup each butter and honey
1 teaspoon each rose water
   and salt
1/2 teaspoon black pepper
Rub mixture, both inside and
out, over:
4-pound chicken (or goose)
Turning to brown all sides,
roast in a 425° oven until
golden. Lower heat to 350° and
add to pan juices:
1 pound fresh apricots, pitted
   and halved
2 tablespoons honey
1 tablespoon sugar
Baste chicken and apricots
with juices and continue
roasting 20 minutes or until
tender. Remove to heated platter,
pour juices over and sprinkle
with:
1/2 cup toasted slivered almonds
   or chopped pistachio nuts
Serves 6-8

PSOMI ROLO ME FETA
Feta Cheese Buns

Make batter for:
Pain Ordinaire (page 6)
Combine:
3/4 pound feta cheese, crumbled
3 tablespoons chopped parsley
1 tablespoon chopped fresh dill
After first rising of dough,
divide dough into 2 dozen balls
and roll each 1/8- to 1/4-inch thick
to make 4- to 5-inch discs. Put
about 4 teaspoons of feta
mixture on each, fold over
opposite ends and pinch together.
Place seam side down on greased
baking sheet, shaping ovals
evenly. Prick with tines of
fork, brush with water and bake
in a 400° oven for 10 minutes or
until golden.
Makes 24

SPANAKOPITTA
Spinach Rolls, An Appetizer

Cook, squeeze dry and finely
chop:
**2-1/2 pounds spinach (or
    combination of spinach,
    Swiss chard, chicory)**
Set aside.

Heat in pan:
2 tablespoons olive oil
Sauté until onions are soft:
1/2 cup minced onion
**1/4 cup each minced green
    onions and parsley**
2 tablespoons minced fresh dill
Add cooked spinach and:
1/2 pound feta cheese, crumbled
1 cup low-fat cottage cheese
3 eggs, beaten
1/4 cup bread crumbs
1 tablespoon lemon juice
1 teaspoon salt
**1/4 teaspoon each pepper and
    nutmeg**
Butter one at a time (see
directions for Phyllo, page 17):
10 sheets phyllo dough
Cut sheets in half, and spread
1/4 cup spinach mixture on lower
edge of narrow end, leaving
1-inch margins. Fold over once,
then fold in side edges and roll
like jelly roll. Repeat with
rest of sheets and filling.
Place seam side down on baking
sheet and brush with:
melted butter
Bake in a 400° oven 15-20
minutes until golden. May be
made ahead of time and frozen.
Makes 20

GREECE

SALATA
Salad

Arrange on salad plate:
Romaine lettuce
tomatoes
Sprinkle with:
olive oil in which a garlic clove
   has marinated 24 hours
red wine vinegar or lemon juice
black pepper
salt
Garnish with:
chervil
parsley
Greek olives
green pepper slices
capers
green onions, slivered
watercress
cucumbers
anchovy filets

ANGINARES
Artichokes

Prepare 6 artichokes as
directed on page 75. Serve with
one of following sauces.

AVGOLEMONO
Lemon Sauce

Beat until frothy:
2 eggs
Beat in:
1 tablespoon flour
1/2 teaspoon salt
1/4 teaspoon pepper
1/4 cup lemon juice
Gradually whisk in:
2/3 cup hot stock or
   artichoke liquid
Cook and stir without boiling
until thickened. If too thick,
thin with a little more stock.

SKORDALIA
Garlic Sauce

Boil until soft:
3 medium potatoes
Peel and mash potatoes,
then add:
3-4 garlic cloves, pressed
1/2 teaspoon salt
1/4 teaspoon pepper
Add alternately, drop by drop:
2 tablespoons lemon juice
6 tablespoons olive oil
Thin with stock if desired.

Both of these sauces are also
good with fish and eggs, and
will keep well to be eaten
cold. They do not reheat
without curdling.

KOTA MELITZENES
ME SPITISIRS HILOPITES
Chicken with Eggplant

Sauté 3 minutes in:
2 tablespoons olive oil
2 garlic cloves, minced
1 sprig rosemary
Add and brown on all sides:
2 fryers, cut up
Transfer all to ovenproof
casserole.
To sauté pan add:
2 tablespoons olive oil
Sauté 5 minutes:
1 unpeeled eggplant, cut in
    1-inch cubes
1 onion, diced
Add:
6 ripe tomatoes, peeled and
    quartered
1 teaspoon each oregano and salt
1 tablespoon sugar
1/4 teaspoon black pepper
1 2-inch piece stick cinnamon
Heat through and add:
1/2 cup dry white wine
Add mixture to casserole.
Bake in a 325° oven 1 hour.
Serve with freshly cooked egg
noodles (page 11) or Pilaf
(page 14).
May be made ahead of time.
Serves 6-8

BAKLAVA
Walnut Honey Dessert

Combine:
1-1/2 cups walnuts, coarsely
    ground
1/2 cup sugar
1 teaspoon cinnamon
In a well-buttered shallow baking
dish approximately 12x8 inches,
place 1 sheet of **phyllo dough**
(page 17).
Brush well with:
melted butter
Repeat with 2 more sheets,
folding in any overlapping
edges. Sprinkle with 1/3 of
walnut mixture; alternate
layers of 3 sheets of buttered
phyllo and walnut mixture; end
with 3 phyllo sheets. Cut into
squares or triangles and bake
in a 375° oven 45 minutes
or until golden. Pour evenly
over assembled layers:
1/2 cup honey
Let cool before removing from
dish. Serve at room temperature
or reheat briefly in a 350° oven.
Serves 8-10

MEDITERRANEAN

CULTURE, commerce, trade and fancy food around the Western Mediterranean suffered a cruel blow when Rome fell. Food became scarce as feudal bickering followed the orderly glory that was Rome. Lord and vassal, potentate and peasant often shared the same basic fare. Civilization from the East took a detour through North Africa to the Iberian peninsula where Moslem empire builders introduced a new religion, new customs and new foods.

With the demise of their empire the Romans undoubtedly consumed more *posca* (vinegar and water) and less *calda* (spiced wine and water); more salt fish, bread, olive oil and less fresh fowl, fish and meat, seasoned with the Roman "soy sauce," *garum* (a brew of salted fish gills, intestines and whole small fish putrefied in the sun, strained and blended with spices, herbs, oil, vinegar, honey and wine); more *pulmentarium* (stew of dried lentils, peas or beans), and fewer fresh cultivated fruits and vegetables. Though some say dried noodles were introduced to the West by Marco Polo from China in the 1200's, others reason that noodles were of earlier Roman origin because it was during the bleak centuries that humble pasta began to blossom into vermicelli, ravioli, spaghetti, cannelloni, pastina, lasagna, fettucine, macaroni, tagliatellini, agnolotti, anolini, tortellini and cappelletti.

While Italian politics progressed through great city-states and various "Holy Roman Empires" to final unification in 1870, peasants were changing the Latin word *minestrare* (to put food on the table) into the classic hodge-podge soup, *minestrone*. Venice, the watery merchant republic, was developing showy delicacies from the Adriatic Sea's scampi, eels, octopus, squid and cuttlefish that have long survived the commercial decline that occurred when da Gama and Magellan found sea routes to the Indies. Genoa, a land of former pirates and freebooters on a sea (the Ligurian) with fewer fish, ended up with a less ostentatious cuisine. Milan's Po River valley became noted for rich cheeses and tender young veal, Florentine chefs imported to Paris by Catherine de Médici are credited with triggering France's fabulous culinary art. Around Florence, a Renaissance hotbed of intellectuals—Machievelli, Michelangelo, Dante, Petrarch and Boccaccio—one today finds simple foods like fennel-scented sausage, *cacio pecorino fresco* (soft, fresh sheep's milk cheese) purported to have the "savor of a first kiss," also spit-roasted *porchetta* (pork) as well as sage-pork on mild white bread, the peasant's sandwich. In Italy butter is favored in the north, olive oil (but not "oily" dishes) in the south. There's more *risotto* and *polenta*, not so much *pasta*, in the north. The use of tomatoes, brought from America in the 1500's, evolved slowly, but now southern Italy's rich, red, tasty tomatoes and its tomato paste are the envy of all Europe.

Switzerland retains from Roman times the Latin *Helvetia* (on its stamps) and shares three other languages with neighbors along with parts of their cuisines. Its freedom-loving people, however, take an independent approach to both language and food. Just ask any German who tries to understand *Schweizdeutsch*. Swiss steak isn't Swiss, but Swiss chard, dating back to 350 B.C., is. So is *muesli* (porridge), *erdapfel suppe* (earth apple or potato soup) and *spiessli* (butter-soaked fillets of beef, pork and veal cooked on skewers interspersed with chicken and ham). Then of course there's Swiss cheese—in fact, an array of them starting with *emmentaler*, *gruyère* and *glarus*. Not so familiar as *fondues* are *raclettes*, chunks of cheese set close to the fireplace and scraped as they melt for eating with tiny boiled potatoes, marinated onions and pickles. The hearty soups, *quiches* and other plain, delicious foods found in Switzerland's many farms and small towns, prove that Swiss "lake dwellers" know how to eat well just as they did in the Stone Age when dough of bruised grain was cooked on rocks under hot ashes.

The *cordon bleu* master chefs of France need no introduction; their culinary masterpieces are world famous. One wonders, however, whether it was these great chefs or the fertile French fields which inspired the thrifty peasant farmers to become master chefs, too. Although this provincial fare is plainer, it also deserves worldwide recognition. Like their *haute-cuisine* cousins in the kitchens of expensive restaurants, the people of France recognize that sincere cooking is hard work, yet fully worth it. Many of them are perfectionists, whose relative prosperity rests primarily on utilizing every scrap of land and food in the best possible way. In 1845 Edmond About wrote of a financially ruined family's servant whose "probity turned into cunning and sorcery." She would borrow bones, then return them to the butcher after extracting by boiling "a mountain of jellied stock and a jar of fat that was better than butter." This enterprising woman should surely have been named the patron saint of all the world's peasants.

So many French peasants did master the alchemy of cooking that all one can do in a lifetime is nibble at the edges of their array of delicacies. Cabbages stuffed with unique, local concoctions; varyingly seasoned pork liver and pigs feet; *matelote* of carp, eel and trout; fresh vegetable soups enriched with wine, garlic, bacon and sausages; a thousand seafood soups and stews; *terrines*, *pâtés* and *rillettes*; mushrooms, *cepes* and game; fresh-picked vegetables glistening with farm butter; *galettes* and pancakes and hot breads from country flour; *pot-au-feu*; *la garbure*; poached eggs with yolks "blushing through precisely cooked whites"; and cheese *beignets* (fritters)—to mention but a few.

Uniquely different from the mainstream of French cooking, is the food on the Mediterranean isle of Corsica. The basic use of chestnuts in the Corsican cuisine is a legacy from the Middle Ages. At that time foreign administrators were exacting imports in tons of grain; the independent and ingenious Corsican peasants simply stopped growing grain and planted chestnut trees. The chestnut, either whole or ground into flour, has been used ever since in *beignets*, porridge, preserves, sausage, *polenta* served in warm slices with *broccio* (cheese) and pork-and-fennel-flavored soup. From the pigs and pig/wild-boar crossbreeds which feed on this beautiful island's chestnuts, acorns, cyclamen bulbs and aromatic wild roots, pork, sausage and ham is produced with a very special flavor.

Another fascinating and individual approach to the Gallic tradition is found in Basque cooking. This clannish group probably settled on the French-Spanish border in prehistoric times, yet remained isolated by the mountainous terrain from the cultural or culinary traditions of either France or Spain. Their language is unlike any other. The Basques did adopt many foods of the area, but fiercely believe that theirs is the only and best way to prepare them. Seafoods, soups and stews are a vital part of the Basque diet, but these shepherds *extraordinaire* excel in dishes of lamb and sheep's milk cheese. Eggs, too, are an important part of the cuisine. The outstanding *piperade* is made from sweet peppers, tomatoes and onions with creamy eggs added at the last minute; another is *oeufs maritchu*, artichokes with an unusual sauce and scrambled eggs.

The Iberian peninsula could harbor the Basques in isolation for so many centuries because its rugged terrain inhibited communication. Likewise no grand national cuisine developed in Spain or Portugal; each area still vehemently promotes its own special dishes. Rich and poor alike, however, share a common respect for food, because the topography and erratic climate often make food, fodder and fuel scarce. Phoenicians, Carthaginians, Romans, Germanic tribes, Goths, Moors and Burgundians all have "invaded" this complex land, some to build, some to destroy; some to settle, some merely to enjoy. Its diverse peoples and climates, its mountains, plateaus, rivers, valleys, coastal plains, and especially its miles upon miles of seashore all contribute to the complexity of its diet.

Phoenicians arriving in 1100 B.C. colonized the west coast, now Portugal, and introduced chickpeas, garbanzos, as well as spices from the East Indies. *Sopa de garbanzos* in various forms is still a mainstay of Spanish diets; spices are used rather sparingly in Spain, more profusely in Portugal. **Sugarcane**, new food taboos and rice arrived with the Moslems around 700 A.D., along with the stable government, much needed irrigation and eastern culture. Meanwhile peasants were developing their "national dish," *olla podrida* (literally "rotten pottage") a stew, of many variations but always containing *garbanzos* and pork. Originally this stew would simmer for days over a fire. As it was consumed, odds and ends were added and bacteria multiplied until people became sick or couldn't stand the stench, at which point the stew would be discarded and a new pot started.

The Moors were finally pushed back to Morocco by the Christians, but Andalusia, Spain's southern province, retains a strong Moslem influence. Here pork is rarely eaten, dishes are light, salty and moist, and the refreshing cold soup *gazpacho* makes eating a pleasure even in hot, glaring weather. Taken from the Arabic word meaning "soaked bread," this drinkable food was known to the Greeks and Romans and is mentioned in the Old Testament, but surely the ancients never enjoyed such imaginative variations of *gazpacho* and tasty garnishes as are found in Spain today.

On the central plateau of Spain, foods are heavier with stronger flavors. Because feed is scarce, whole roasted lambs, young veal and suckling pigs are often favored over matured mutton, beef or pork. On the Levantine eastern shore where rice is grown, the well-known *paella*, cooked in the two-handled frying pan for which it's named, has as many recipes as there are cooks. Its appeal is based on the ability of rice, a truly universal food, to absorb and retain the flavors of seafood, tomatoes, peppers, herbs and spices without number.

An ingredient often used in *paella* is *chorizo*, a long-cooked sausage made with pork, herbs, spices, paprika and garlic. The range of delicious seafoods from Mediterranean to Atlantic to Bay of Biscay (where the Moors never settled) defies description, though sardines do abound. Mountain cave-ripened cheeses of Celtic origin and corn adopted from the New World add zest and nourishment in the northwest provinces. Eggs, almonds, parsley, garlic and olive oil are important everywhere.

Portugal's fare is characterized not only by more spices but also by more cream and butter. Throughout history the seafaring Portuguese have brought back occasional wives and children from all corners of the world along with exotic foods to enrich and broaden its gastronomy. Even today shiploads of cod are gathered and salted by its fishermen with great effort and danger at the Grand Banks off Newfoundland.

Morocco, Algeria and Tunisia (named Barbary states after the wandering Berbers of old), the lands of the Moors, now are inhabited as well by Spaniards, Jews and Turkish Moslems and a fair number of Frenchmen. Through the years the poorest North African peasants have lived on bread dipped in olive oil. Luckily, a tastier fare predominates. Flexible enough to be eaten alone, as a dessert or as a main dish with varied accompaniments, *couscous* is made from pellets of wheat middlings, semolina or other grains moistened with water and oil, then steamed over meat and vegetables. Dishes like this are eaten from a common bowl with pre-washed fingers of the right hand.

In Tunisia, raw, tart crabapples and hot seasoning are relished. Bread sticks of plain flour, salt and water, *kaaki*, in many shapes are hawked to blunt hunger pangs. Although alcohol is a Moslem taboo, *boukha*, a very sweet fig brandy, is available for the religiously uninhibited. It's served with brined, fresh vegetables for contrast. *Tajines*, one-pot dishes, as in so many other countries, depend for their excellency on the ingenuity of the cook and the ingredients he or she collects.

There's more French influence in Algeria. Fruit-flavored meat and excellent fresh vegetables predominate along the coast; grain and grazing animals are more important on the interior plateau.

Moroccans tend to prefer lighter seasoning. *Mechoui* (whole roasted lamb), chicken, fruits, vegetables and *pastilla* (salted pie of lamb, eggs, pigeon, chicken, vegetables and spices) are always accompanied by minted hot tea in the Muslim tradition.

The varied effects of history and local economics, the flow of peoples and their conflicts, the relative productiveness of climate, soil and sea, have never been more dramatically demonstrated than by the array of peasant foods found in the profusion of Mediterranean cultures.

ITALY

ZUPPA DI VONGOLE
Clam Soup

Bring just to boil:
2 tablespoons olive oil
1 garlic clove, minced
1-1/2 cups tomato juice
1/2 teaspoon oregano
6 sprigs Italian parsley*
Add:
4 dozen small clams,
   well scrubbed
Cover and steam over high heat
5 minutes, or until clams open.
Serve in individual bowls with
crusty bread.
Serves 4

MINESTRONE
Vegetable Soup

Soak overnight:
1 cup kidney beans
Sauté until soft in:
1/4 cup olive oil
3 onions, sliced
3 carrots, sliced
4 ribs celery, sliced
1 teaspoon salt
1/4 teaspoon each black pepper
   and sage
Transfer to large kettle
and add:
3 quarts water or stock
drained kidney beans
1 6-ounce can tomato paste
3 zucchini, sliced
4 potatoes, sliced
1/2 pound Italian green beans,
   cut up coarsely
Bring slowly to boil, cook
with lid tilted for 2 hours or
until beans are tender. Bring
back to boil and add:
1 cup rigatoni or mostaccioli
Cook, stirring to prevent
sticking, until pasta is
al dente (page 17). Cool and
refrigerate.
Next day reheat and adjust
seasonings.
Serve with Grissini (page 7),
grated cheese and Pesto.
Serves 8-10

PESTO
Basil Sauce

In mortar and pestle crush:
1-1/2 cups fresh chopped
   basil, firmly packed
4 garlic cloves, finely minced
3 tablespoons minced
   Italian parsley* (optional)
1/2 cup pine nuts
Gradually stir in:
1 cup olive oil
Add:
1/2 teaspoon salt
1/4 teaspoon nutmeg
3/4 cup grated Parmesan
   cheese or half Romano and
   Pecorino* cheese
Can be refrigerated in closed
glass jar up to one week, or
freeze in ice cube tray and use
as needed.

PASTA AL PESTO
Noodles with Basil Sauce

Cook as directed:
1 recipe Noodles (page 11)
Toss with:
2 tablespoons butter
To **Pesto** sauce add:
**1/2 cup water in which noodles
were cooked**
Toss into noodles and serve
immediately. Pass grated
Parmesan or Pecorino* cheese.
Serves 8

VEGETABLES
To Deep Fry the Italian Way

For the batter, beat:
4 egg yolks
1/4 cup grated Parmesan cheese
Fold in:
4 egg whites, stiffly beaten
Dip large stems of Swiss chard
that have been blanched (page 17)
1 minute and drained, or 8 large
squash blossoms or zucchini, or
eggplant in batter and fry. Try
other vegetables.

CECI CON FINOCCHIO
Garbanzo Beans with Fennel

Combine:
**2 cups garbanzo beans, soaked
overnight and drained**
1-1/2 quarts water
1 teaspoon salt
Simmer 2 hours or until tender.
Drain and reserve liquid.
Sauté 5 minutes in:
2 tablespoons olive oil
1 garlic clove, minced
1 onion, chopped
**2 cups chopped fennel,
including tops**
**1/2 teaspoon each oregano, thyme
and black pepper**
Add to garbanzos with:
**1/4 pound salt pork, rinsed
and sliced**
**enough reserved liquid to
cover beans**
In bean pot, covered, bake in
300° oven 2 hours. Better made
a day ahead and reheated.
Serves 6-8

SPAGHETTI ALLA MARINARA
Spaghetti with Fresh Tomato Sauce

Sauté until soft and golden in:
3 tablespoons olive oil
1 cup minced onions
4 garlic cloves, finely minced
**1/2 pound fresh mushrooms
(optional), sliced**
Add and cook 10 minutes:
**2 pounds ripe tomatoes, peeled
and cubed**
**2 tablespoons chopped
fresh basil**
1 teaspoon each salt and sugar
1/4 teaspoon black pepper
Pour over:
**1 pound spaghetti freshly
cooked al dente (page 17)**
Sprinkle with:
**grated Parmesan
or Pecorino* cheese**
If desired add to sauce last
5 minutes of cooking:
3 anchovies, cut up
Serves 4

ITALY

SALSA DI POMODORO
Basic Tomato Sauce

Brown in:
2 tablespoons olive oil
2 garlic cloves, minced
1 onion, minced
1/2 pound sliced mushrooms
   (optional) or
1/2 cup dried mushrooms,
   soaked until soft and
   minced
Add and simmer, uncovered,
1-1/2 hours:
3 cups ripe tomatoes,
   peeled and chopped
1 6-ounce can tomato paste
3/4 cup water
3/4 cup red wine
1 tablespoon sugar
1 teaspoon each salt, oregano
   and minced fresh basil
1/2 teaspoon each rosemary and
   black pepper
1/4 teaspoon cinnamon
1/2 teaspoon finely minced
   lemon peel
1/2 cup chopped Italian parsley*
Last 10 minutes, add if
desired:
1 pound ground beef,
   sautéed quickly
Makes 4 cups

MALFATTI
Spinach-Ricotta Balls

Blanch (page 17) 1 minute:
1 large bunch fresh spinach
Drain, squeeze out *all* excess
water and mince. Combine with:
2 cups ricotta cheese
2 eggs, beaten
1/3 cup grated Parmesan cheese
1 cup bread crumbs
1 tablespoon finely minced
   fresh basil
1/2 cup finely minced green
   onions and tops
2 garlic cloves, finely minced
1 teaspoon salt
1/4 teaspoon each black pepper
   and nutmeg
Mix to form stiff mixture;
chill several hours. Form into
small 1/2 teaspoon ovals and
cook in gently boiling water.
When malfatti rise to surface
they are done. Remove with
slotted spoon and keep warm.
Cover with:
Basic Tomato Sauce,
with or without meat.
Serves 6-8

ITALY

POLENTA CON SALSA DI POMODORO
Polenta with Tomato Sauce

Prepare recipe for:
Cornmeal (page 7)
Slice and cover with:
Basic Tomato Sauce (page 66),
with or without meat.

SPAGHETTI CARBONARA
Spaghetti with Egg and Bacon

Sauté:
2 ounces pancetta (Italian bacon) or Canadian bacon, diced
Cook al dente (page 17):
1 8-ounce package spaghetti
Drain and immediately stir in:
the pancetta
2 tablespoons of the drippings
1 egg, beaten
Mix well so the hot spaghetti cooks the egg. If desired add:
butter
grated Parmesan cheese
Pass coarse black pepper.
Serves 2-4

LASAGNE CARNIVALE
Green Lasagne

For the white sauce, melt until bubbly:
1/4 pound butter
Sprinkle with:
1/2 cup flour
Cook and stir 3 minutes without browning. Gradually add:
3 cups hot milk
Cook and stir until smooth and thickened. Cool and add:
1/2 teaspoon nutmeg
Set aside.

Brown:
1/2 cup each minced carrot and celery
Add:
1 recipe Basic Tomato Sauce (page 66),
adding the meat if desired.
Set aside.

Cook as directed:
1 recipe Green Noodles (page 11)
Cut in 1-inch strips, drain and cool on wax paper, to prevent sticking.

Have ready:
8 slices ham, halved
1 pound pork sausage, cooked and sliced
2 cups fresh peas
5 hard-cooked eggs, sliced
1/2 cup black olives
1-1/2 cups grated Parmesan or Monterey Jack cheese (or half of each)

In a 9x13-inch casserole, layer tomato sauce, lasagne, cheese, ham, peas, eggs, olives, sausage and white sauce.
Repeat layers, ending with white sauce and topping with cheese.
Bake in a 350° oven 40 minutes.
Serves 8-10

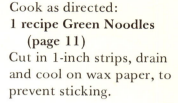

FINOCCHIO
Baked Fennel with Cheese

Bring to boil:

2 quarts water

**1 teaspoon each salt and
    olive oil**

Add and boil 3-5 minutes or until
tender-crisp:

**3 medium fennel (with stalks),
    halved or quartered**

Drain and reserve 1/2 cup liquid.
Place in a single layer in a
shallow buttered baking dish.
Pour reserved liquid over and
top with:

**2 cups grated Monterey
    Jack cheese**

Sprinkle with:

1/2 cup grated Parmesan cheese

Bake in a 375° oven to melt
cheeses and brown slightly.

Serves 6

FRITTATA MOSCA
Omelet of the Flies

Beat until frothy:

5 eggs

Add:

1/4 cup bread crumbs

**3 tablespoons grated Parmesan
    or Pecorino* cheese**

**1/2 teaspoon each fresh
    thyme and salt**

1/4 teaspoon black pepper

In iron skillet heat:

2 tablespoons butter

Pour egg mixture into skillet,
pulling edges away from sides
with a fork as egg congeals.
When bottom is golden, cover
skillet with flat lid, turn upside
down, slide omelet back into
skillet, adding more butter if
needed. Cook until golden and
set. Serve with salad of tuna fish,
hard-cooked eggs and minced
celery. Frittatas can also be
made with zucchini, spinach,
precooked and halved small
artichokes, leftover meats or
poultry.

Serves 2-4

BRANZINO AL VINO
Sea Bass in Wine Sauce

Clean, dry thoroughly and
set aside:
**2 pounds sea bass (or other
firm white fish)**
Sauté 5 minutes in saucepan:
2 tablespoons olive oil
1 onion, minced
2 anchovy filets, mashed
1 tablespoon chopped parsley
Add and simmer 20 minutes:
**3/4 cup each dry white wine and
fish stock (or clam juice)**
Dredge fish in:
flour, salt and pepper
In skillet brown
fish on all sides in hot oil.
Lower heat and cook 5 minutes
or until tender. Pour sauce over
and garnish with chopped
Italian parsley*.
Serves 4

ANITRA RAGU
Braised Wild Duck

Wash and dry thoroughly:
2 wild ducks
Rub inside and out with:
2 garlic cloves, crushed
Sprinkle with:
2 tablespoons flour
In heavy pot brown duck on
all sides in:
1/4 cup butter
Add:
1 cup chopped onions
1/2 cup chopped olives
1/4 cup chopped parsley
1 cup red wine
**1/2 teaspoon each rosemary, sage
and black pepper**
1 teaspoon salt
1/2 cup pine nuts (optional)
Cover and simmer 45 minutes or
until duck is tender. Transfer to
heated platter, pour juices over
and serve with freshly made
Polenta (page 7) and green
salad, dressed with oil and
vinegar.
Serves 4

BACCALA E POLENTA
Salt Cod and Polenta

Soak overnight in several
changes of water:
2 pounds salt cod
Drain, remove bones and cut up.
Add to:
**Basic Tomato Sauce without
meat (page 66)**
Cook 20 minutes until tender
and serve with freshly made
Polenta (page 7).
Serves 8

ITALY

RISOTTO CON CALIMARI
Rice with Squid

Follow directions for
Risotto (page 14).
Omit mushrooms and for the
mushroom liquid substitute:
fish stock or clam juice
Just before serving add calimari
mixture.

Sauté in:
2 tablespoons butter
3 tablespoons minced green onion
2 garlic cloves, finely minced
1/4 cup minced Italian parsley*
Raise heat and add:
2 pounds squid, cleaned, well
    dried and cut into 1/4-inch
    rings
Cook and stir 4-5 minutes until
just tender. Squid toughens if
cooked too long.
Serve risotto with
grated Parmesan
lemon wedges
Serves 4-6

POLPOTTE
Meat Patties

Combine:
1/2 pound each ground beef
    and veal
1 tablespoon each minced Italian
    parsley* and fresh grated
    lemon peel
1 garlic clove, minced
1/2 teaspoon salt
1/4 teaspoon each black pepper
    and nutmeg
2 tablespoons bread crumbs
1 egg, beaten
Shape into 4 patties and brown
on both sides in a little butter.
Any of the following may be
added as a variation:
finely minced onion and/or
finely minced mushrooms
Or:
1 cup chopped spinach,
    blanched (page 17) 1 minute
    and well drained
1/2 teaspoon fresh basil,
    chopped
Serve with buttered fresh Green
Noodles (page 11).
Serves 4

PANETTONE
Fruit Bread

Prepare one recipe of:
Basic Sweet Bread Dough
    (page 8)
After first rising, turn out on
floured board and knead in:
1/2 cup each diced citron, white
    raisins and dark raisins
Shape into 2 round loaves, place
on greased baking sheet and
let rise until double in bulk.
Brush with:
2 tablespoons melted butter
Bake in a 400° oven
10 minutes. Lower heat to 350°
and bake 30 minutes. Remove from
oven and brush with more melted
butter to keep crust soft.
Makes 2 loaves

FRANCE

POT AU FEU

French version of broth, meat and vegetable meal. A family soup, it varies widely in different locations.

Bring to boil:
4 quarts water
1 beef knuckle bone
1 3-pound beef rump
Skim off any scum that rises to the top, cover and simmer 1-1/2 hours.
Then add:
1 chicken, cut up
1 pound chicken giblets
1 pound marrow bones, sawed
 into 1-inch lengths, blanched
 (page 17) 5 minutes and
 wrapped in cheesecloth
3 carrots, cut in chunks
3 leeks, white only,
 cut into chunks
2 onions, quartered
2 turnips, quartered
3 celery ribs, sliced
 thickly on diagonal

Bring to boil, cover and simmer 45 minutes or until chicken is tender. Unwrap marrow bones and place on large platter with the beef, the chicken and the giblets. Surround with vegetables and keep warm. Serve the strained and defatted broth with separately cooked pasta or rice and toasted bread. Serve the meat and vegetables with pickles and horseradish. In many parts of France pork, lamb, mutton and/or veal are substituted or added. May be made ahead of time. Serves 8-10

ANGUILLE
AUX FINES HERBES
Eels with Herbs

Sauté, stirring, 5 minutes in:
4 tablespoons butter
2 cups shredded lettuce
1 cup chopped sorrel
1/2 cup chopped parsley
3 tablespoons each chopped
 fresh chervil, sage and
 tarragon
Add and simmer, covered, 10 minutes:
1/2 cup dry white wine
Bring to boil and add:
2 pounds eel, cut into
 1-inch pieces
Cook, covered, 10 minutes or until done. Season to taste with:
salt and pepper
Beat in:
2 egg yolks, beaten
Cook without boiling until slightly thickened. Serve with:
lemon wedges
Serves 4-6

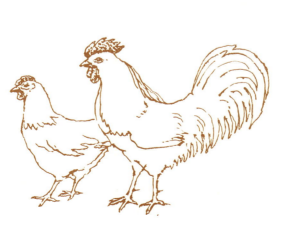

FRANCE

FAISAN
Pheasant

Combine:
2 tablespoons softened butter
2 garlic cloves, minced
1/2 teaspoon thyme
Rub well into underside and
outside of:
**1 young pheasant, halved
   lengthwise**
Sprinkle generously with cracked
pepper and lightly with salt.
Roast in a 450° oven skin
side down for 10 minutes. Turn
and continue cooking 20-30
minutes until tender. Remove to
heated platter and deglaze (page
17) with:
1/2 cup dry white wine
Heat to reduce slightly and pour
over pheasant. Serve with fresh
whole mushrooms sautéed
in butter.
Serves 2-4

POULARD RÔTIE
Roast Chicken

Sprinkle inside and out with:
salt and pepper
**1 3- to 4-pound roasting.
   chicken**
Roast in a 450° oven 40-50
minutes or until tender. Remove
to heated platter and deglaze
(page 17) pan with:
1/2 cup dry white wine
Reduce by half, pour over
chicken and garnish with
fresh watercress.
Serves 4

RIS DE VEAU BRAISÉS
Braised Sweetbreads

Soak 1 hour in cold water
to cover:
**2 pairs calves' sweetbreads
   (about 1-1/2 pounds)**
Drain and add:
fresh cold water to cover
2 slices lemon
1 teaspoon salt
Bring to boil and cook
5 minutes. Drain and reserve
liquid. Separate cooled
sweetbreads into bite-size
pieces, removing any tough
membranes. Set aside. In a
2-quart ovenproof pot melt:
2 tablespoons butter
Add and cook, stirring to
brown lightly:
1 onion, chopped
1 carrot, thinly sliced
1 strip bacon, diced
2 tablespoons minced parsley
1/4 teaspoon tarragon
Add:
sweetbreads
1 cup reserved liquid
1/4 cup dry white wine
1 teaspoon salt
1/4 teaspoon black pepper
1 bay leaf
Bake in a 375° oven
45 minutes until sweetbreads
are browned and vegetables
tender. Sprinkle generously with
minced parsley and serve with
plain rice.
Serves 4

CHOU FARCI
Stuffed Whole Cabbage

Parboil about 5 minutes or
until limp:
1 large curly Savoy cabbage
Combine:
**1 pound each lean ground pork
    and veal**
1 cup finely minced ham
2 garlic cloves, minced
1 teaspoon salt
1/2 teaspoon black pepper
Starting at center of cabbage
and working toward outer leaves,
stuff mixture throughout leaves
and in the center, omitting
the two outer leaves. Shape
cabbage to original size and tie
firmly with string. In large
ovenproof casserole heat:

2 tablespoons butter or oil
Brown 5 minutes:
2 onions, sliced
Add:
4 carrots, sliced
2 turnips, sliced
2 cups stock or water
1 bay leaf
1/2 teaspoon thyme
Place cabbage in casserole,
cover and cook in a 275° oven
2-3 hours or until cabbage is
cooked through. Test by piercing
with fork. Last 10 minutes of
cooking add:
1 pound fresh peas
Place cabbage on heated
serving platter surrounded by
vegetables, cut into wedges to
serve and pass plenty of:
Pain Ordinaire (page 6)
May be made ahead of time.
Serves 6-8

POIREAUX ET LAITUE
Braised Leeks and Lettuce

Layer bottom of large
saucepan with:
uniformly sized leeks
**small whole heads of lettuce or
    lettuce cut in quarters
    or eighths**
Add:
1/2 cup stock
salt and pepper
dots of butter
Cover and cook over low heat
for 20-30 minutes until tender.
Celery, endive, spinach,
cabbage or any combination
may be cooked this way. Add
more water to non-leafy
vegetables.

FRANCE

CRÊPES
French Pancakes

Sold in small shops all over
France, made to order as you
watch with almost any kind of
filling you desire.
Prepare **Crêpes** (page 13).
Fill with one of the following:
**eggs scrambled with cheese,
    sautéed onions, marjoram,
    salt and pepper
leftover minced meat or
    seafood in gravy or sauce
sautéed minced mushrooms
    in sauce
Basic Tomato Sauce with meat
    (page 66)**
Sprinkle with grated Parmesan
cheese after filling and rolling,
and serve immediately. Or arrange
rolls, not touching, in buttered
baking dish, pour more sauce
over, sprinkle with cheese and
bake in a 350° oven to heat
through.
For dessert sprinkle with:
**powdered sugar and melted
    butter and/or jam**

TARTE À L'OIGNON
Onion Tart

Line a 9-inch flan pan or
pie plate with:
**Hot Water Pastry (page 13)
    rolled 1/4 inch thick**
Sauté 5 minutes in:
**3 tablespoons butter
3 cups thinly sliced onions**
Remove cover and let moisture
cook away. Cool and arrange on
pie crust. Combine and sieve
onto onions:
**3 eggs, beaten
1-1/2 cups half-and-half cream
2 teaspoons flour
1 teaspoon salt
1/4 teaspoon each nutmeg and
    white pepper**
Bake in a 375° oven 40-45
minutes until custard is set
and crust golden. Cool 5 minutes
before serving.
For variation, layer between
onions:
**diced bacon, blanched (page 17)
    1 minute and sautéed in butter
    and/or
sautéed minced mushrooms and/or
grated or sliced Gruyere cheese**
Serves 6

OEUFS À LA OSEILLE/ÉPINARDS
Eggs with Sorrel or Spinach

Sauté until moisture
evaporates in:
**3 tablespoons butter
1-1/2 - 2 pounds sorrel, or half
    sorrel and half spinach,
    cut up**
Mound on:
6 pieces fried bread
Top with:
scrambled, fried or poached eggs
Garnish with parsley and
sliced tomatoes.
Serves 6

POMMES DE TERRE AU BASILIC
Potatoes with Basil

Cook in boiling salted water
until tender:
**young, uniformly-sized
    potatoes, peeled**
Drain and toss in to taste:
**melted butter
chopped fresh basil
salt
white pepper**

ARTICHAUTS ENTIERS BOUILLIS
Whole Boiled Artichokes

Place in saucepan side by side, bottoms down:
6 medium artichokes, trimmed
Add:
3 cups boiling water or stock
1/4 cup lemon juice
1 teaspoon salt
1/2 teaspoon oregano
2 tablespoons olive oil
1 garlic clove (optional)
Bring back to boil, cover and cook over medium heat 30-50 minutes or until tender. Serve hot with melted butter, or cool upside down and serve with oil and vinegar dressing of choice.
Serves 6

CHEESE AND FRUIT DESSERTS

There are numerous dessert cheeses from France:
Neufchâtel (with fruit)
Brillat-Savarin (with fruit)
Coeur à la Crême (with wafers or fruit)
Petit Suisse (with wafers and/or fruit)
Croissant Demi-Sel (with wafers and/or fruit)
Camembert (fruits, especially pineapple and/or grapes)
Crême Chantilly (fruits and berries, especially strawberries)

The best fruits to serve with cheese are pears, apples, grapes, berries (with creamy mild cheese), tangerines and assorted nuts in the shell. Always serve cheese and fruit at room temperature.

IBERIAN PENINSULA

ROUGAIL DE MORUE
Salt Cod Appetizer

Soak overnight:
1/2 pound dry salt cod
Drain, discard skin and bones
and shred cod with fingers.
Sauté until liquid has
evaporated (about 5 minutes) in:
3 tablespoons olive oil
1 onion, chopped
1 cup chopped tomatoes
1 chili pepper (page 17), minced
the salt cod
Remove from heat and toss in:
2 tablespoons chopped
  fresh coriander*
1/4 teaspoon black pepper
Eat hot with Pain Ordinaire
(page 6) or Broa (page 10) or
cold with lettuce. Pass lemon
wedges.
May be made ahead of time.
Serves 4-6

COLIFLOR AL AJO
Cauliflower with Garlic

Cook until tender-crisp in
salted water and lemon juice:
1 head cauliflower
Meanwhile sauté in:
3 tablespoons olive oil
4 teaspoons minced garlic
1 teaspoon vinegar
1/8 teaspoon cayenne pepper
Place cauliflower in bowl
and sprinkle with sautéed garlic.
Serves 4-6

SOPA DE AJO
Garlic Soup

Sauté until golden in:
3 tablespoons olive oil
3-4 tablespoons minced garlic
Add and simmer 10 minutes:
6 cups boiling water
Place in 6 bowls:
6 pieces dried bread
Pour soup over bread and serve
with sliced tomatoes sprinkled
with minced raw garlic. Or,
place the bread in 6 greased
ovenproof bowls, top with 1 egg
and bake in a 350° oven
5 minutes. Pour hot soup into
bowls and serve.
Serves 6

ELZEKARIA
Basque Soup

Soak overnight:
1 cup navy or haricot beans
Sauté until soft in:
2 tablespoons bacon drippings
1 large onion, sliced
2 garlic cloves, minced
1 small cabbage, shredded
Add:
drained beans
2 thick slices bacon, diced
6 cups water
Bring to boil, cover and simmer
2 hours. Add salt to taste and
serve with Broa (page 10).
Pass vinegar and the peppermill.
Often a tablespoon of vinegar
is added to each bowl.
May be made ahead of time.
Serves 6-8

SOPA DE CEBOLLA
Onion Soup

Sauté until soft in:
3 tablespoons olive oil
2 Spanish onions,
    coarsely shredded
Add and simmer 10 minutes:
6 cups boiling water
1/2 teaspoon salt
Beat together:
2 eggs
1 tablespoon vinegar
Whisk 1/2 cup hot soup into eggs, gradually add this mixture to rest of soup and serve with dried bread. Pass the peppermill.
Serves 4

SOPA DE BERRO
Potato-Watercress Soup
from the Azores

Sauté until soft in:
3 tablespoons olive oil
1/2 cup minced onion
2 garlic cloves, minced
Add:
4 cups meat or chicken stock
1-1/2 cups diced potatoes
1 bunch watercress, chopped

Cover, bring to boil and simmer until potatoes are soft. Purée and add:
2 cups milk
2 cups diced ham
Reheat and serve with Broa (page 10).
May be made ahead of time.
Serves 6-8

ZARZUELAS DE PESCADO
Fish Stew

To prepare broth, lightly sauté in:
1/4 cup olive oil
4 garlic cloves, minced
1/2 cup diced onion
1/2 cup minced red or green pepper
2 cups chopped ripe tomatoes
Add and bring to boil:
1/2 cup each water and
    dry white wine
Add:
6 fillets of sole, halibut or
    other firm white fish
Cook gently until fish is just done. Remove fish to heated serving platter, pour sauce over and sprinkle with:
3 tablespoons roasted chopped
    almonds
minced parsley
Serve with hot, fluffy white or brown rice.
Serves 6

TERNERA RELLANA
Stuffed Breast of Veal

For stuffing combine:
1/2 pound lean pork butt,
    ground
1/4 pound ham, minced
1/2 cup each grated carrot,
    milk and bread crumbs
1 egg, beaten
2 tablespoons chopped parsley
1/4 teaspoon black pepper

Place on board, meat side down:
1 3- to 4-pound breast of veal
Spread stuffing on veal, roll tightly and tie with string.
In Dutch oven brown in:
3 tablespoons olive oil
1 onion, chopped
2 garlic cloves, minced
Push aside and brown veal roll on all sides. Then add:
1 cup stock
1/2 cup sherry
Bring to gentle boil, cover and simmer 1-1/2 to 2 hours, adding more stock or water if needed. Remove string and serve with pan juices. Potatoes, carrots, turnips or cabbage may be added half way through cooking.
May be made ahead of time.
Serves 4-6

IBERIAN PENINSULA

PESCADO ASADO AL HORNO
Baked Fish

Line a large baking dish with:
sliced ripe tomatoes
thinly sliced onions
chopped parsley
Drizzle over:
olive oil
Place on top:
1 large fish, cleaned,
    (head left on), or
    fish fillets
Repeat layers of tomatoes,
onion, parsley and oil,
sprinkling lightly with:
salt and pepper
Bake in a 350° oven 20-40
minutes depending on size of
fish. Garnish with watercress
and serve with cauliflower
(page 76).

TORTILLA DE PATATÁ
Potato Omelet

Brown in:
2 tablespoons olive oil
1 onion, diced
Add:
2 cups diced, cooked potatoes
3/4 cup leftover meat,
    vegetable or seafood,
    sausage or combinations
Heat and add:
4 eggs, well beaten
1 teaspoon salt
Mixture should cover entire
skillet. Brown over medium heat
until eggs are set. Flip over
onto heated serving plate and
serve as a main luncheon or
supper dish with salad of
lettuce, chicory, watercress
and minced celery. Pass the
peppermill.
Serves 4
Dessert omelets can be made
the same way with fruits such
as oranges, melon, pineapple.

PAO DE LÓ
Sponge Cake

Beat until light:
6 egg yolks
2 whole eggs
Gradually add, beating until
very thick:
3/4 cup sugar
Gradually add and beat until
smooth:
3/4 cup sifted, unbleached flour
Pour into a 9-inch square
cake pan lined with buttered
wax paper. Bake in a 325°
oven 30 minutes or until done.
Let cool 5 minutes before
turning out onto rack.
Optional: add 1/2 teaspoon
vanilla, lemon or almond
flavoring to batter.
Serves 6

HARIRA
Moroccan Vegetable Soup

Similar to couscous, a soup
rather than a stew. Ingredients
vary according to location
and pocketbook.
Soak overnight:
1/2 cup garbanzo beans
Brown in:
3 tablespoons olive oil
**1 pound lamb, cut in 1/2-inch
  cubes**
Add:
soaked garbanzo beans
1/2 cup lentils
2 quarts water
1 lamb bone
1 onion, chopped
2 tomatoes, chopped
**1/2 teaspoon each turmeric
  and powdered ginger**
1 teaspoon paprika
**3 tablespoons chopped
  fresh coriander***
Bring to boil and simmer
1-1/2 hours. Stir in and cook
10 minutes:
1/2 cup vermicelli
Beat together:
2 eggs
1 tablespoon lemon juice
Remove from heat and
immediately stir slowly into
soup to make strands. Serve
with Pita (page 7).
Serves 6

SLATA MECHONIA
Moroccan Salad

Combine and simmer, covered,
5 minutes:
**2 large onions, cut in
  1/2-inch dice**
**1 cucumber, peeled, seeded and
  cut into 1/2-inch dice**
**1 sweet red pepper or bell
  pepper, cut into 1/2-inch
  dice**
**3 ripe tomatoes, peeled and
  cut into 1/2-inch dice**
1/2 cup water
Remove from heat, strain and
discard liquid. Place in bowl
and add:
2 garlic cloves, finely minced
1/3 cup olive oil
3 tablespoons lemon juice
1/2 teaspoon salt
**1/4 teaspoon each black
  pepper and cumin powder**
**1/4 cup chopped fresh
  coriander***
Chill and serve on lettuce
leaves. Scoop up with:
Pita (page 7)
Serves 6

NORTH AFRICA

COUSCOUS
Moroccan Stew

Soak overnight and drain:
1 cup fava or garbanzo beans
Place in large stew pot with:
3 pounds lamb (leg or shoulder
with some fat) or half lamb
and half chicken
2 medium carrots, cut in
2-inch lengths
2 onions, quartered
2 turnips, quartered
1/2 cup thick tomato purée
1 slice fresh ginger root
6 whole cloves
1 2-inch stick cinnamon
1 teaspoon each saffron,
ground coriander seed
and salt
1/2 teaspoon black pepper
3 cups water
Bring to gentle boil, cover
and simmer 1-1/2 hours. Last
20 minutes of cooking add:
2 zucchini, cut in 2-inch
lengths
1/2 cup raisins, plumped
(page 17)

Soak in cold water 5 minutes:
2 cups couscous (see below)
Drain and spread on tea towel
to swell for 20 minutes. Place
in top of couscoussière (or
steamer lined with cheesecloth).
Steam for 10 minutes, turn out
on large platter and rub gently
by hand to separate grains.
Return to couscoussière or
steamer and steam 10 minutes.
Toss with:
1/4 cup softened butter
Mound on heated serving platter
and surround with meat
and vegetables.
Serve with Arissa Sauce.

ARISSA SAUCE
Extremely Hot Sauce

Combine:
2 tablespoons cayenne pepper
1 tablespoon cumin powder
1/2 teaspoon salt
If desired, add and cook,
stirring 5 minutes:
1/2 cup olive oil
Serves 6

COUSCOUS DOUGH

Couscous is a semolina cereal
product imported from Algeria
and is sold in Middle Eastern
stores. It can also be served
as a dessert sprinkled with
cinnamon and sugar.

To make your own, have ready:
1-1/2 cups farina or semolina
9 tablespoons water
3/4 cup unbleached flour
Place on a large platter or tray
1/2 cup of the farina; using one
hand for water, the other for
flour, gradually sprinkle 1/3 of
the water and flour, alternately,
onto the farina. Rub with palms
of hands in circular motion
until mixture is broken up and
makes small grains. Repeat
process twice and spread the
grains out to dry.
Makes 2 cups

QODBAN
Lamb Kidney and Heart

Soak in cold salted water
1 hour:
**2 pounds lamb kidneys
and hearts**
Clean and cut into chunks.
Marinate at least 4 hours in
mixture of:
**1/4 cup each lemon juice and
olive oil**
2 garlic cloves, finely minced
1 teaspoon salt
**1/2 teaspoon each black pepper,
turmeric, powdered ginger
and cumin**
Skewer and broil over hot coals
8 minutes per side. Garnish
with parsley. Can also skewer
mushrooms and/or green pepper
chunks, blanched (page 17)
30 seconds, with the meat cubes.
Serves 4

BRIK
Deep-Fried Meat Turnovers

Sauté until meat is no
longer pink:
1/2 pound ground lamb
1 cup minced onion
2 garlic cloves, minced
Add and cook until moisture
is gone:
**2 medium tomatoes, peeled
and chopped**
1/2 teaspoon salt
1/4 teaspoon black pepper
Add:
**2-3 tablespoons chopped
fresh coriander***
Cool mixture. Adjust seasonings
to taste and place 2 tablespoons
on each of 12 round **Egg Roll
Skins** (page 12). Spread the
filling to make a ring. Into center
of each break 1 egg.
Quickly fold over to make
half-moon shape, sealing edges
with a little water, and fry in
deep oil at 400° until golden,
turning once. Drain on paper
toweling and serve immediately.
Makes 12
Serves 4-6

CIGARS
Moroccan Dessert

One at a time, cut into
8 rectangles:
phyllo sheets (page 17)
On long edge of each rectangle
place:
1 tablespoon ground walnuts
1/2 teaspoon sugar
Roll, tucking in side edges,
to make a "cigar." Seal seam
with a tiny bit of water. Drop
a few at a time, seam side
down, into hot oil. Fry until
golden, drain on paper toweling
and sprinkle while hot with:
powdered sugar
cinnamon
Makes 8

Germany
Czechoslovakia
Austria
Hungary
Romania
Yugoslavia
Bulgaria

CENTRAL EUROPE

O THE sensitive Celts dwelling along the Danube in 400 B.C. the Roman conquerors were barbarians. The Celts soon realized, however, that the Romans had much to offer and were slowly assimilating the new culture when the "real" barbarians interrupted from the north. Ever since, the lands from the Black Forest to the Black Sea have been ravaged by wave after wave of conquerors from every direction—Teutonis, Alemannis, Franks, Huns, Vandals, Slavs, Goths, Saxons, Jutes, Angles, Bulgars, Lombards, Charlemagne, Magyars, Crusaders, Tartars, Mongols, Turks, Napoleon, Nazis, Russians—bent on pillage, carnage and rape, or at the very least adventure. Some merely destroyed and left; some settled down; all left marks. There must be a Celtic resilience built into the river, for Danube peoples through the years have retrieved many good things from their hectic past, especially in matters of food.

Even the most ruthless invaders had foods of some interest. The scraped raw meat of the marauding Tartar horsemen from Mongolia in the 13th Century, for example, evolved into Steak Tartar with the addition of raw egg yolk, green onions and condiments; its cooked counterpart, developed in the city of Hamburg, is now a favorite of millions. Another famous food—sauerkraut—might not have reached Germany were it not also for the Tartars who adapted it (by adding salt) from the winter fare of workers on the Great Wall of China. The northern Chinese had for years lived during the summer on fresh chopped cabbage and rice wine, which they preserved by souring for the winter. Sauerkraut with its valuable vitamin C subsequently became an important dish for European sailors, and the Germans served it sautéed in fat, caraway, onions and pork. Today's *schlactplatte* (butchers' platter) is a tempting variety of smoked meats and sausages with sauerkraut.

Sausages are believed to go back to the New Stone Age reaching Austria, then Germany, via the Greeks and Romans. One sausage, the wiener (from the word Vienna) or frankfurter (from Frankfurt), needs no introduction to the world's "peasants" of today. Germans, ever since the early bow-and-arrow Germanic tribes wandered south from the Baltic, have been great eaters of beef and pork. Oxen of the field, hogs and other game of the forest traditionally were roasted whole on spits over open fires and devoured boisterously with much beer and chewy dark bread of rye, barley or buckwheat. Game is still available in Germany, for forests were never denuded like those on Mediterranean shores by man, sheep and goat. German tastes, unlike Roman did not run to fish, olive oil, white bread and wine. The *braten* (roast), whether cooked in a pot or in the oven, is still king. Two hundred breads are baked in West Germany today, and even more varieties of bland or spicy sausages are available. In these cooler climates milk stayed fresh long enough for cream to rise and be churned into butter. It wasn't necessary to sour the milk or make cheese immediately as it was farther south. Caraway and poppy seeds were the popular seasonings until the hot Indian spices found their way to central Europe with the coming of the East-West sea trade of the Middle Ages. The chicken, that jungle fowl eaten in India as early as 600 B.C., also found its way to Germany as a food to join native ducks and geese. But that important vegetable now eaten boiled, fried or mashed, in pancakes, hot or cold salad, dumplings, bread or cake didn't become popular until two hundred years after it arrived from the Americas—and then only by the 1740 decree of Frederick II of Prussia. Famine was upon the land, so the king ordered everyone to plant potatoes. Perhaps typical of their temperament the German people responded dramatically to this edict and made the potato their most important vegetable. It has remained so ever since.

Meanwhile farther down the Danube somewhat different food patterns developed as various tribes arrived on the scene. Slavs from the Polish-Russian border, people so oppressed that their name was used to form the word "slave," sought better hunting, better grazing for their cattle, and land easier to till with their forked sticks. Soon some were pushed west into Bohemia by Asian nomads and became known as Czechs from the language they spoke. Their culinary legacies are the fabulous sausage and dumplings, Prague ham and other Czechoslovakian specialties.

Vienna, more than any other city, seems to have followed the Celtic tradition of absorbing many good things from all the cultures thrust upon it and developed a truly international cuisine. For example, "Vienna little cuts," or *Wiener Schnitzel*, now world-famous, are thought to have originated in Milan.

The Asian influence in Hungary is much more pronounced. The wandering milk-and-meat shepherds, the Magyars, liked Hungary's eastern plains so well they settled down and grew wheat. Formerly these nomads had boiled down cubes of meat with onion in a kettle over an open fire, dried them in the sun and carried them along on their wanderings in a sheep-stomach bag for boiling into stew or soup. In their new homeland, they soon prepared this national dish, *gulyas*, from fresh ingredients. They continued, however, to grill much of their beef and lamb over open fires and still make the long-keeping nomadic *tarhonya*, a paste of flour, salt and eggs crumbled then dried in an oven. Some say the key to the best Hungarian dishes in lots of onions fried beforehand exactly right in fresh pork fat; others say it's the proper use of the ground, dried, ripe, sweet red peppers, *paprika*, supposedly introduced by the Turks, but probably brought to them from America as recently as the 18th century.

Yugoslavia in a way is a microcosm of Central Europe, a mixture of four cuisines, three religions, two alphabets, three languages, six republics and two autonomous provinces. Near the sea Venetian-style fish and olive oil dishes are outstanding. In the foothills one finds Austro-Hungarian dishes like schnitzels; along the Danube, Byzantine delicacies; and in the central mountains, dishes with Turkish influence. Its people like their strong-flavored, heavy, spicy peasant dishes, like the Bosnian delight *musaka* (roasted minced meat and vegetables served with a thick sauce of milk and beaten eggs).

The Bulgars, contributing yoghurt for health and long life, and the Slavs, their language, long ago intermarried and settled down in what was once part of the Roman Empire. In their diet Bulgarians place less importance on meat than their neighbors and more on their exceptionally good rice, *oriz*, other grains, nuts and vegetables. Sunflower oil is more important than butter, lard or mutton fat, but cheeses of sheep's milk are as popular as in the rest of the Balkans. Many of Bulgaria's foods are close to those of Greece.

Romanian peasants really put their hearts into cooking. They're especially ingenious in adapting foods to their own use—foods from everywhere, not only from Rome for whom their country is named and under whose close influence they lived from 1 to 271 A.D. The peasants obviously recognized a nourishing food in corn when it arrived from America in the 16th century. A Romanian staple is *mamaliga de aur*, or maize bread of gold, revered as one of God's special gifts when drizzled with butter, yoghurt or sour cream. But nourishment is not their only consideration.

Their interest in flavor and variety is apparent in their wide use of herbs and in a mixed charcoal grill, for example, of *mititei* (homemade skinless sausages) served with pig's kidney, liver and brains; chops, loins, ribs and fresh sausage of pork; calf's udder, French fries, sour cabbage and sharp red peppers. *Ghivetch* is a vegetable-and-herb melting pot, and the *ciorbas* (sour soups of fermented wheat bran, sauerkraut juice, meat, eggs, etc.) are said to improve with age. Presumably the homemade *tzuica* (plum brandy) which the peasants call apa *chiora* (cross-eyed water) does, too. In addition to corn the Romanians grow great quantities of eggplant for use in their version of *musaca* (layers of eggplant, meat, sliced tomatoes cooked in soup stock).

From the Danube's headwaters in the Black Forest to its lush delta near the Black Sea, the great river flows through lands where the mighty struggles that have enslaved many people in the past have forged fierce pride in their heritage not the least of which is "barbarian" foods of the ages.

MÜSLI
Swiss Breakfast Favorite

Combine and refrigerate
overnight:
1 cup each milk and rolled oats
Place in two bowls and serve
with any or all:
wheat germ
toasted almonds, walnuts or
  filberts
raisins
fresh apples, grated
fresh berries or other
  sliced fruit
honey or brown sugar
Pour milk over and eat!
Serves 2

RETTICH SALAT
White Radish Salad

Combine and chill:
4 cups coarsely grated
  white radishes
6 tablespoons oil
2 tablespoons vinegar
2 tablespoons mayonnaise
  (optional)
2 teaspoons Dijon-style mustard
1 teaspoon sugar
2 tablespoons minced parsley
salt and pepper to taste
Serves 4-6

LATTICH UND SPECK
Lettuce and Bacon

Trim and blanch (page 17)
3 minutes:
6 small heads Romaine lettuce
Drain well and set aside. Cook
until crisp:
8 thick slices bacon, diced
Pour off all but 1 tablespoon of
drippings and add:
1 cup minced onion
2 tomatoes, peeled and chopped
2 tablespoons chopped parsley
1/2 teaspoon thyme
Cook until onion is tender and
add reserved Romaine. Sprinkle
with:
1/2 teaspoon salt
1/4 teaspoon white pepper
Cover and cook until lettuce is
tender-crisp, adding stock if too
dry. Remove cover and boil away
any moisture. Serve with Rösti
and fresh fruit dessert.
Also good with roast meats
or poultry.
Serves 6

RÖSTI
Fried Potato Cake

Cook 10 minutes, cool and
refrigerate 8 hours:
2 pounds medium potatoes
Peel potatoes and shred with
coarse grater (special graters
available). Then add:
1/2 cup shredded onion
  (optional)
In skillet heat:
1/4 cup butter or oil
Add potatoes and sprinkle with:
1/2 teaspoon salt
Press into a flat cake the size
of skillet and cook over medium
heat 25 minutes or until bottom
is crusty, adding more butter
or oil as needed. Sprinkle with:
2 tablespoons cream
Dot with:
1/4 cup sweet butter
Continue cooking 10 minutes.
Flip over onto hot serving
plate crusty side up, surround
with pan-fried sausage slices,
sliced sautéed onions, and
thickly sliced homemade bread.
Also good with fried eggs or
melted cheese.
Serves 6

SWITZERLAND

KÄSE RUBREI
Egg and Cheese Bake

Combine:
6 eggs, beaten
1/3 cup milk
1/2 teaspoon salt
1/4 teaspoon each white pepper
    and tarragon
2 tablespoons melted butter
In skillet heat:
3 tablespoons butter
Add eggs, cook and stir until
starting to set, pour into
buttered casserole and
sprinkle with:
1 cup finely minced cooked ham
    or sausage, or leftover meat
4 ounces Gruyère cheese, grated
1/4 cup bread crumbs
Bake in a 400° oven 10 minutes
or until golden. Serve with
green salad and small, unpeeled
new potatoes boiled tender-crisp
in a small amount of stock and
dressed with melted butter and
minced parsley.
Serves 4

KÄSESCHNITTE MIT SCHINKEN
Open-Face Sandwich

Fry bread in butter until golden,
top with crisp fried bacon and
a slice of Gruyère cheese.
Broil to melt cheese and top
with tomato slices and
a fried egg.

NEUE KARTOFFELN MIT RAHM QUARK
New Potatoes with Cottage Cheese

Rahm Quark is a form of cottage
cheese, not available here, but
similar to a mixture of yoghurt
and smooth cottage cheese.
Mix to taste:
unflavored yoghurt
cottage cheese
Add:
chopped chives
paprika
Serve on boiled new potatoes
with sliced salmon and salad.

FLEISCHKÄSE
Meat Loaf

Soak in:
1/2 cup milk
2 slices whole wheat bread
Purée in blender:
1/2 cup red wine
1 carrot, cut up
1 small bell pepper, cut up
1 celery rib, cut up
1 onion, cut up
2 parsley sprigs
Add to soaked bread with:
1/2 pound each ground veal
    and lamb
1 pound ground chuck
1 teaspoon salt
1/2 teaspoon black pepper
1/2 cup chopped mushrooms
    (optional)
Mix together well, put in loaf
pan and bake in a 350° oven
1 hour. Serve hot. Or cool,
slice, sauté on both sides in
butter, and serve with pickles
and a fresh green salad.
Serves 6

BUTTERMILCH-SUPPE (KALT)
Cold Buttermilk Luncheon Soup for hot day

Combine:
1 quart buttermilk
1 slice pumpernickel,
   crumbled (1/3 cup)
1/4 cup sugar
2 tablespoons lemon juice
1/2 teaspoon grated lemon rind
1/2 cup raisins
Let stand 1 or 2 days to thicken.
Adjust seasonings with sugar and
lemon and serve very cold.
Serves 4

BUTTERMILCH-SUPPE
Buttermilk Soup

Bring to boil:
1 quart milk
Very slowly, stirring
constantly, add:
3/4 cup farina
Return to boil, lower heat and
continue cooking 10 minutes or
until very thick.
Add:
1/2 cup raisins or cooked pears
brown sugar or honey to taste
2 cups buttermilk
Heat without boiling and serve
as a light Sunday night supper.
Serves 4-6

SCHWÄBICHE SPÄTZLE
Noodle Dumplings

Into a measuring cup break:
2 eggs
Add water to measure 1 cup.
Transfer to large bowl and
beat until well blended.
Gradually beat in:
2 cups unbleached flour
1/2 teaspoon salt
Beat until bubbly and elastic.
Have ready a large pot of
boiling salted water, a bowl of
cold water and a buttered baking
dish. Place a large fine-mesh
strainer in the boiling water.
Wet a small cutting board
(special boards are available
with a handle and thinner end
edge) and place about 1/4 cup
of batter on board. With table
knife spread a portion of batter
to end of board to make thin
coating. Dip knife in cold water
and, dipping frequently, shred
batter into boiling water to
make small strands. Use all
batter on board and let this
portion boil 1 minute. Lift
strainer to drain and place
spätzle in baking dish. Repeat
with rest of batter.
Pour over batter:
1/4 cup melted butter

Reheat in a 350° oven and
serve with:
bratwurst, potato salad and
sauerkraut or frankfurters and
lentils (in cream sauce with
vinegar to taste).
Serves 6

Leftover spätzle
To each 1-1/2 cups add:
1 egg, beaten
1 teaspoon each chopped
   parsley and chives
1/4 teaspoon salt
1/8 teaspoon pepper
Place in greased casserole, dot
with butter, sprinkle with
grated Parmesan cheese and bake
in a 350° oven 20 minutes
or until egg is set.

GERMANY

RINDERBRUST
Roast Beef

An optional ingredient in this recipe is:
1 large onion, unpeeled, baked at 400° for 30 minutes
In large kettle place:
5-pound lean beef brisket or rump
1 pound chicken giblets, necks and/or backs
2 small onions each stuck with 2 cloves
6 celery ribs and tops, chopped
3 carrots, chopped
6 parsley sprigs
1 thyme sprig
10 peppercorns
pimientos (optional)
1 teaspoon salt
1 garlic clove
2-4 cups cold water to almost cover

Bring to boil, cover and simmer 2 hours, skimming off any scum that rises to surface. Remove beef and set aside. Strain the stock, return the meat and add:
the baked onion
Bring back to boil, cover and simmer 1 hour or until meat is tender.
The last 20 minutes of cooking, add cut-up vegetables such as:
carrots
turnips
parsnips
rutabagas
red bell peppers
Serve meat sliced, surrounded by vegetables, and sauce of stock thickened with cornstarch. Pass applesauce which has been sieved and seasoned to taste with:
orange juice
freshly grated horseradish
Good with Bratkartoffeln or Salzerkartoffeln which follow
Serves 6-8

BRATKARTOFFELN
Fried Potatoes and Onions

Fry until well browned in:
shallow layer of lard or bacon drippings
thinly sliced potatoes
thinly sliced onions

SALZERKARTOFFELN
Boiled Salt Potatoes

Boil potatoes in strongly salted water until tender. Peel and drain. Serve with melted butter and minced parsley, dill, onion, caraway or bread crumbs mixed with bits of ham or bacon.

HAFERFLOCKEN-CROQUETTES
Oatmeal Croquettes

Combine:
1 cup rolled oats
**3/4 cup hot water or
    scalded milk**
Let stand 1 hour and add:
1 egg, beaten
1/2 cup chopped onion
1/2 teaspoon salt
1/8 teaspoon pepper
Mix well and drop by teaspoons
into skillet containing:
1/4 cup hot oil
Brown on each side, drain on
paper toweling and serve hot
with fried egg, ham, bacon or
sausage.
May also be served with any
roast and gravy.
Serves 4-6

HIRSCHBRUST
Venison Stew

Combine, bring just to boil
and cool:
2 cups red wine
2 tablespoons oil
**1/2 teaspoon each rosemary,
    thyme and peppercorns**
3 whole cloves
1 teaspoon sugar
2 parsley sprigs
1/2 cup celery tops
Pour wine mixture over:
**3 pounds venison meat, cut
    into cubes**
Marinate overnight, drain and
reserve marinade.
In Dutch oven or stew pot brown
meat on all sides over high
heat in:
3 tablespoons oil
Add and brown:
2 onions, sliced
1 carrot, grated
1/2 pound mushrooms, sliced

Sprinkle with:
2 tablespoons flour
Cook and stir 3 minutes.
Then add:
reserved marinade
1 cup water or beef broth
1 sprig rosemary
1 bay leaf
1-1/2 teaspoons salt
1/2 teaspoon black pepper
2 tablespoons minced parsley
Bring just to boil, cover and
simmer 1 hour or until tender.
Serve with plain boiled or
mashed potatoes. Or potatoes
cooked in beef broth with
onion, then dressed with butter
and minced parsley.
May be made ahead of time.
Serves 10

GERMANY

SCHWEINEBRATEN IN BIER
Roast Pork with Ale

Combine:
1 tablespoon flour
1 teaspoon dry mustard
3/4 teaspoon salt
1/4 teaspoon black pepper
Rub mixture into:
3-pound pork loin roast
Put rack in roasting pan
and add:
12 ounces ale or dark beer
1 onion, chopped
Place pork loin on rack and
roast in a 400° oven
20 minutes. Lower heat to 325°
and continue cooking until pork
is done, about 2 hours in all.
Baste frequently with pan
drippings after heat has been
lowered. Serve with Lentils with
Prunes, and Red Cabbage.
May be made ahead of time.
Serves 6

LINSEN MIT BACKPFLAUMEN
Lentils with Prunes

Combine:
1 cup lentils
2-1/2 cups water
Bring to boil, cover and simmer
1/2 hour or until tender.
Add:
1 cup pitted prunes, cut up
1 teaspoon salt
1/2 teaspoon black pepper
Cook over low heat 15 minutes to
blend flavors. May be made
ahead of time.
Serves 6

ROTKOHL
Red Cabbage

Sauté until soft:
2 slices bacon, diced
Add:
**2 cups pared, diced
cooking apples**
4 cups shredded red cabbage
2 tablespoons vinegar
1/4 cup water
1/2 cup dry red wine
1 tablespoon sugar

Bring to boil, cover and simmer
15 minutes or until cabbage is
tender. Adjust seasonings to
taste with salt and pepper.
Serves 6

NUDELN MIT SCHINKEN
Noodles with Ham

Cook until tender:
4 ounces wide noodles
Place half on bottom of buttered
shallow baking dish.
Sauté until soft in:
2 tablespoons butter
1 cup chopped onions
Add to noodles and sprinkle
with:
1 cup ground ham
Cover with rest of noodles and
pour over all:
1 cup buttermilk
Sprinkle with:
3/4 cup grated Münster cheese
Bake in a 350° oven 20 minutes
or until heated through and
cheese is melted. Serve with
cooked kale or Brussels sprouts
dressed with buttered
bread crumbs.
Serves 4

WURSTBEGRABNIS
Burial of the Sausage

Sauté in:
fat
sauerkraut
onions
caraway seeds
Alternate in layers with:
sliced cooked sausages
Cover with:
mashed potatoes
Bake in a 350° oven 15-20
minutes to heat through and
brown top.

KNOLLEN-SELLERIE
Celeriac Relish

Peel and cut into 1/2-inch dice:
1 pound celeriac (celery root)
Boil in salted water 5 minutes
until just tender crisp. Dress
with:
Hot Salad Dressing (page 16)
Serves 4-6

STOLLEN
Fruit Bread

Combine and let stand at least
1 hour:
1/2 cup each white raisins,
    currants and blanched,
    slivered almonds
1 cup mixed candied fruits
2 tablespoons brandy
Make:
Basic Sweet Bread Dough (page 8)
After first rising turn out
on floured board and knead in
above fruit mixture. Divide
in half and roll each into
a 1/2-inch thick oval. Fold over,
place on greased baking sheet
and let rise 20 minutes. Brush
with melted butter and bake in
a 375° oven 30 minutes. Brush
with more melted butter to keep
crust soft. Sift powdered sugar
over while still hot and again
when cool.
Makes 2 large loaves

MÜRBETEIG
Fruit Tart

Combine until crumbly:
1/2 cup cold butter
1/4 cup cold shortening
2 cups unbleached flour
1 teaspoon baking powder
1/3 cup sugar
1/4 teaspoon salt

Blend in:
1 egg, beaten
1 tablespoon milk
Let dough rest 1 hour.
Press into a 10-inch Mürbeteig
tart tin (special tin with ridge
in center; substitute a pie
plate), prick bottom with fork
and bake in a 375° oven
40 minutes. Turn out onto
serving plate and let cool.

While baking, combine:
1/2 cup puréed strawberries
1/2 cup each sugar and water
2 tablespoons cornstarch
Cook and stir until thickened.
Cool. Fill pastry shell with:
1 quart whole fresh strawberries
Spread strawberry purée over
and serve at room temperature
with or without whipped cream.
As a variation cover shell with:
cooked sliced apples
mixture of bread crumbs,
    sugar and cinnamon
Serve with:
whipped cream
May be made ahead of time.
Serves 8

AUSTRIA

BRIES-SUPPE
Sweetbread Soup

Soak in ice water 30 minutes:
2 or 3 pairs veal sweetbreads
Trim, slice and set aside.
Brown in:
2 tablespoons butter
2 onions, thinly sliced
3 tablespoons minced shallots
3 carrots, sliced
Sprinkle with:
2 tablespoons flour
Cook and stir 3 minutes or until
roux starts to turn golden.
Then add:

6 cups chicken stock
3 potatoes, sliced
Bring to boil, stirring to blend
roux, cover and simmer 1/2 hour.
Then add:
1 small cabbage, shredded
1 teaspoon salt
1/4 teaspoon white pepper
reserved sweetbreads
Bring back to boil and cook over
medium heat 10 minutes. Adjust
seasonings to taste and sprinkle
with:
minced parsley
This may be served as a main
meal or luncheon dish.
Serves 4-6

LINSENSALAT
Lentil Salad

Combine:
1 quart water
2 cups lentils
1 bay leaf
2 parsley sprigs
1 sliver lemon peel
Cook until beans are tender but
still retain their shape, about
20 minutes. Drain, discard bay
leaf, parsley and lemon peel
and set aside.

Combine:
2 tablespoons salad oil
**1 tablespoon each vinegar and
    sugar**
**1/2 teaspoon each salt and
    black pepper**
1 small onion, finely minced
Mix with lentils and serve
hot or cold with sliced tomatoes
and boiled beef.
Serves 4-6

GRÖSTL
Hash

Sauté until crisp in:
half lard and half oil
leftover meat
potatoes, sliced
onions, sliced
Season with:
salt and pepper
minced chives or chervil
Serve with fresh vegetable
or salad.

WIENER SCHNITZEL
Cutlets

Pound until paper thin:
6 thin veal, pork or
   venison cutlets
Dip in a combination of:
1 egg, beaten
1 teaspoon lemon juice
Coat with mixture of:
bread crumbs
salt and white pepper
paprika
Chill at least 30 minutes.
Sauté quickly on both sides
until crisp in:
half lard and half oil
Do not overcook.
Serve with lemon wedges,
buttered fresh asparagus and
noodles, or with cold potato
salad and shredded cucumbers
dressed with vinegar.
Serves 6

BETTELMANN
Beggar's Pudding

Combine:
1/3 cup bread crumbs
2 cups applesauce
1/4 cup raisins
2 tablespoons chopped almonds
2 eggs, beaten
Pour into 4 buttered custard
cups and top with mixture of:
2 tablespoons each brown
   sugar and bread crumbs
1 teaspoon butter
1/8 teaspoon cinnamon
Bake in a 350° oven
20 minutes until top is golden.
This may be eaten either warm
or cold.
Serves 4

CZECHOSLOVAKIA

**POLEVKA Z HOVEZI
OHANKY
Oxtail Soup**

Prepare and set aside:
2 cups fresh noodles (page 11)
Combine and bring to boil:
**2 quarts water
3 pounds oxtails, cut up
2 teaspoons salt
1 onion, chopped
2 carrots, chopped
2 ribs celery and tops, chopped
3 parsley sprigs, chopped
2 parsley roots*, scraped
   and sliced
6 peppercorns
6 whole allspice
2 bay leaves**

Lower heat, cover and simmer
until oxtails are tender. Remove
oxtails and keep warm. Strain
broth and adjust seasonings with:
salt, pepper and sugar to taste
Bring back to boil with:
**2 carrots, sliced
2 onions, cut in eighths
2 celery ribs, sliced on
   diagonal**
Cook until vegetables are
almost tender and add:
**1/4 pound thinly sliced
   mushrooms
1 pound fresh peas**
Cook until mushrooms and peas
are just tender.
Add:
cooked fresh noodles
Heat and sprinkle with:
1/2 cup chopped parsley
Serve with the oxtails
on a separate plate.
Serves 8

DUSENE ZAMPIONY
Sautéed Mushrooms

Slowly sauté over medium
heat in:
**1/4 cup butter
1 pound fresh mushrooms, sliced
1 teaspoon caraway seeds
1/2 teaspoon salt**
When tender, raise heat to
cook away moisture. Serve with
mashed potatoes and veal stew.
Serves 6

KYNUTE KNEDLIKY
Yeast Dumplings

Dissolve in:
1/2 cup warm water
1 tablespoon dry yeast
Add:
1 teaspoon sugar
1 teaspoon Wondra flour*
Blend well and set aside
10 minutes.
Stir in:
3 eggs, well beaten
Gradually beat in:
1 teaspoon salt
2 cups Wondra flour
Beat vigorously, using large
upward strokes to let air into
batter. After thoroughly
mixed add:
1/2 cup more Wondra flour

Continue beating at least
15 minutes, scraping bowl often,
until dough is smooth and satiny
and makes air blisters. Cover
bowl with dampened tea towel and
let rise in warm place until
double in bulk, about 30 minutes.
Taste for salt, adding if
needed, and turn out onto board
floured with:
1/2 cup Wondra flour
Knead until dough no longer
sticks, adding as little
additional flour as possible.
Form into 2 large or 4 small
ovals and let rise in warm place
30 minutes, turning occasionally.
Drop into a large kettle of
boiling salted water filled
2/3 full; cook at medium boil
30 minutes for large, 20 minutes
for small dumplings. Turn once
and test with toothpick before
removing with slotted spoon.
Place on platter and immediately
prick in several places to
release steam. Working quickly,
cut into 1/2-inch slices; to do
so without crushing, slip thread

under dumpling, cross thread
ends and pull upward in a quick
crisscross action. Serve
immediately with entrée of
choice. Or cool and fry slices.
Can be reheated wrapped in
foil (350° oven).
Serves 8-10

KYNUTE HOUSKOVE KNEDLIKY
Yeast Dumplings with Croutons

Prepare dough for:
Yeast Dumplings (preceding recipe)
Sauté until coated in:
2 tablespoons butter
5 slices bread, cubed
Add to dumpling dough after first
rising and proceed according to
basic dumpling recipe.

CZECHOSLOVAKIA

SVICKOVA
Sour Beef

Sprinkle with:
1 teaspoon salt
1/2 teaspoon black pepper
2 teaspoons vinegar
2 tablespoons oil
**1 4-pound eye of round or
rump of beef**
Refrigerate 8 hours or more,
turning often. Over high heat
sear on all sides in:
bacon drippings
Place in baking pan and add:
1 cup water and/or wine
**2 cups chopped celery and
some leaves**
2 carrots, chopped
1/2 onion, chopped
2 bay leaves
Cover tightly and cook in
a 325° oven 2 hours or until
tender, checking occasionally
to see if more liquid is needed
and turning often. Remove meat,
discard bay leaves and purée
vegetables in blender with:

**1 cup liquid from pan (add water
if needed to make 1 cup)**
2 tablespoons flour
Return to pan, heat and adjust
seasonings with:
salt and pepper
Then add:
1/2 pint sour cream
**1-2 tablespoons lemon juice
or to taste**
Slice meat and arrange on
ovenproof platter, pour gravy
over, cool, cover tightly and
refrigerate 8 hours or more. Heat
in a slow oven, covered, and
serve with extra gravy. The
process of slow cooking and
then reheating is the secret
of the flavor. Serve with
Yeast Dumplings (page 97).
May be made ahead of time.
Serves 6

OVOCNE KNEDLIKY
Dessert Dumplings

Follow directions for
Yeast Dumplings (page 97)
increasing sugar measurement to
2 tablespoons. After first rising,
put spoonfuls of dough onto
floured board, flatten with palm
of hand and place in center:
6-8 seedless grapes, or
6 pitted fresh cherries, or
**2 fresh apricots or prunes,
cut up**
Pull dough up and around the
fruit to make a ball. Cook all
together in boiling salted water,
turning once, until puffy,
about 12·minutes.
Serve with:
melted butter and sugar, or
**toasted bread crumbs and
melted butter, or**
**cottage cheese, sugar and
melted butter**
Can be frozen after cooking and
steamed to reheat. Or eaten
cold without the melted butter.
Makes 16 to 20

HABART ZOLD BAB LEVES
String Bean Soup

Combine, cover and cook until
beans are tender-crisp:
2 cups fresh green beans,
   cut in 1/4-inch dice
2 cups water
1/2 teaspoon salt
Melt until bubbly:
2 tablespoons butter
Sprinkle with:
3 tablespoons unbleached flour
Cook and stir at least
3 minutes without browning.
Gradually add:
1 cup milk
the beans and 1 cup of
   their liquid
Over medium heat cook and stir
5 minutes or until smooth and
thickened. Season with:
1 teaspoon minced fresh savory
salt and pepper to taste
Remove from heat and stir in:
1 tablespoon white vinegar
Ladle into soup bowls and
top with:
sour cream
Serve with Peasant Bread
(page 8) and fresh fruit
dessert. May also be
served cold.
Serves 4

BORJU PAPRIKAS TARHONYA
Veal Stew with Egg Semolina

Toss together:
2 pounds veal stew cut
   in 1-inch cubes
2 tablespoons flour
Lightly brown in:
3 tablespoons butter
the veal
2 onions, sliced
1 small bell pepper, chopped
1/2 pound fresh mushrooms,
   sliced
Add:
2 tablespoons paprika
1/8 teaspoon cayenne pepper
1/4 teaspoon black pepper
1 teaspoon salt
1/4 cup chopped parsley
1 cup boiling water
Cover and simmer until veal
is tender. Then add:
1 cup sour cream
Heat but do not boil. Serve
with Egg Semolina.
Serves 6

EGG SEMOLINA

Combine:
2 eggs, beaten
2 cups Wondra flour*
1 teaspoon salt
Turn out on board and knead,
gradually adding sprinklings
of water to make a crumbly
dough that barely forms into
a ball. Let rest uncovered
20 minutes. Grate on medium-
coarse grater, turning and
reforming into ball as you
grate. Dough will tend to
crumble. Spread out on large
board and let dry 2-4 hours.
Pour into 3 quarts rapidly
boiling salted water and cook
30 seconds. Drain, return to
pot and toss in:
6 tablespoons melted butter
Sprinkle with:
salt and pepper to taste
Serve immediately. May
be made ahead of time.
Serves 6

HUNGARY

CSOKOLADE MIGNON
Chocolate Cake Squares

Melt and set aside:
2 ounces bitter chocolate
Cream until fluffy:
1/4 cup sugar
4 tablespoons soft butter
Beat in one at a time:
5 egg yolks
Add:
melted bitter chocolate
1 tablespoon cocoa
Beat until stiff:
5 egg whites
Gradually add while beating:
1/4 cup sugar

Fold into yolk mixture
and blend in:
1/3 cup sifted unbleached flour
3 tablespoons ground walnuts
Pour into greased and floured
8-inch square pan. Bake in
a 350° oven 20-25 minutes
or until cake tests done. Cool
on cake rack. Split into two
layers and fill with
a mixture of:
1/2 cup apricot jam
2 tablespoons rum
Frost with **Mocha Icing.**
Cut into squares before serving.

MOCHA ICING

Combine:
2 tablespoons softened butter
1 tablespoon cocoa
1-1/2 cups sifted powdered sugar
2 tablespoons hot strong coffee
1/2 teaspoon vanilla

TUROS PALACSINTA
Crêpe Dessert

Make **Crêpes** (page 13).
Combine:
1 pound dry cottage cheese
1 egg, beaten
5 tablespoons sugar
1/8 teaspoon vanilla
Spread mixture on crêpes, roll
and place in buttered baking
dish. Sprinkle them with:
1/4 cup sifted powdered sugar
Top with:
any kind of fruit preserves
dollops of sour cream
Heat in a 325° oven 10-15
minutes.
Makes 20

MAJAŚ PAPRIKAS
Chicken Livers with Paprika

Sauté until onions are
golden in:
4 tablespoons butter
1 onion, sliced
1/2 pound mushrooms, sliced
Dust with:
2 tablespoons flour
1/2 teaspoon each salt
    and pepper
1 pound chicken livers
Add to onion and mushrooms
and brown. Then add:
1 tablespoon paprika
1/4 cup white wine
1/2 cup water
1/8 teaspoon cayenne pepper
1/2 cup chopped walnuts
Cover and simmer 10 minutes
until livers are tender.
Beat together and add:
1/2 cup sour cream
1 egg, beaten
Heat but do not boil. Serve
over rice and garnish with
chopped parsley.
Serves 4

PAPRIKAS KRUMPLI
Potatoes

Heat in a skillet:
1/4 cup ham or bacon drippings
Add:
2 large onions, sliced
4-5 potatoes, sliced
1-2 tablespoons paprika
1/2 teaspoon salt
1/4 teaspoon black pepper
Cover and cook, turning
occasionally, until tender and
browned. Serve with baked ham.
Serves 4-6

KUSAPSKI DJUVEC
Yugoslavian Stew

Cut into fourths lengthwise:
1 pound pork kidneys
Remove center membrane and
cut into chunks. Blanch (page 17)
a few minutes in boiling
water with:
half of a lemon
Drain, rinse and drain again.

Dry and combine with:
1 pound lean pork butt,
    cut into 1-inch chunks
3 potatoes, peeled and cut
    into 1-inch chunks
1 large eggplant, peeled
    and cut into chunks
1 large onion, coarsely chopped
3 tomatoes, peeled and
    cut into eighths
2 leeks, chopped
1/2 cup chopped parsley
1 cup each white wine and water
2 teaspoons salt
1/2 teaspoon black pepper
Place in casserole, cover and
bake 1-1/2 hours in a 375°
oven. Sprinkle with:
1 cup grated Monterey
    Jack cheese
Bake, uncovered, 15 minutes.
Serve with Peasant Bread
(page 8) and fresh fruit
dessert.
May be made ahead of time.
Serves 6-8

BULGARIA

SELSKA CHORBA
Celeriac Soup

Bring to boil:
6 cups lamb broth
1 onion, diced
**2 cups grated celeriac
   (celery root)**
1/2 cup raw rice
Cover and simmer 1 hour until
rice and celeriac are tender
and soup is thick. Then add:
2 tablespoons lemon juice
salt and pepper to taste
Serve with plain yoghurt and
minced fresh mint as main
meal with salad. May be made
ahead of time.
Serves 4-6

SHOPSKA SALATA
Simple Salad

Arrange in overlapping circles
on bed of:
finely shredded lettuce
**thinly sliced unpeeled
   cucumbers**
sliced tomatoes
Sprinkle with:
**grated Sirene, Monterey Jack
   or other mild creamy cheese**

DEBABCHA
Grilled Meat Sausages

Combine and blend thoroughly:
**1/2 pound each ground veal
   and beef**
2 garlic cloves, minced
1 teaspoon salt
**1/4 teaspoon each black
   pepper and nutmeg**
**1/2 teaspoon each thyme and
   allspice**
1/8 teaspoon baking soda
2 tablespoons water
Form into 8 3-inch long
sausages. Broil, preferably
over charcoal, for 10 minutes,
turning to brown all sides.
Serve with sauerkraut and
fried potatoes and a garnish of:
minced green onions
sliced radishes
pickles
parsley
Also good as a part of
a mixed grill of liver, kidney,
pork chops and lamb hearts.
Serve with Yellow Summer
Squash (page 103) and rice
(page 15).
Serves 4

SHARAN SAWREHI
Stuffed Carp

Rub inside and out with:
2 teaspoons salt
**1 whole carp (3 pounds
   cleaned)**
Set aside for 2 hours.
Sauté until soft in:
3 tablespoons olive oil
2 cups chopped onions
1 garlic clove, finely minced
1 cup finely chopped walnuts
Soak until soft in:
1/2 cup water
1/2 cup raisins
Add water and raisins to onion
mixture and season with:
**1/8 teaspoon each cayenne
   pepper and black pepper**
Cover and cook 5 minutes.
Remove from heat and gently
stir in:
roe from fish (if available)
Stuff fish and place on heavy
foil. Drizzle with:
3 tablespoons olive oil
Wrap tightly and bake in
a 375° oven 1 hour. Serve
with salad and rice (page 15)
or fresh noodles (page 11).
Serves 6

TOKFOZELEK
Yellow Summer Squash

Sauté 5 minutes in:
2 tablespoons butter
2 pounds yellow summer squash,
   cut in julienne *
1 small onion, minced
1 teaspoon salt
Add:
3/4 cup water
2 tablespoons vinegar
1 teaspoon each sugar
   and paprika
1 tablespoon dill seed
Cover and cook until squash
is tender. Then add and blend
well:
1/2 cup sour cream
Heat but do not boil.
Serves 4-6

BANITZA
Phyllo Yoghurt Dessert

To make filling combine:
2 eggs, beaten
1/2 pound feta cheese, crumbled
6 tablespoons plain yoghurt
3 tablespoons sugar
1/2 teaspoon freshly grated
   lime or lemon peel

See directions for working with:
phyllo dough (page 17)
Melt:
1/4 pound butter
With melted butter, brush
1 sheet phyllo, fold over, cut in
half and place halves, brushing
with more butter, in a buttered
6x9 baking dish. Spread with
3 tablespoons filling, cover with
another sheet treated as above,
and continue until filling is
used up. You will need about
16 sheets in all. Bake in
a 375° oven until top is golden,
turn out on cookie sheet with sides
and score top by cutting into
serving pieces about halfway
through. Bake until top is golden,
cut through into serving pieces and
serve with fresh fruit.

ROMANIA

MUSACA CU CARTOFI
Vegetable-Veal Musaca

Sauté in:
2 tablespoons oil
2 pounds potatoes, sliced
Remove and set aside. In same
skillet sauté:
2 large onions, sliced
1 garlic clove, minced
1 pound ground veal
Sprinkle with:
1/4 cup minced parsley
1/2 teaspoon thyme
1/4 teaspoon fennel seed
Beginning and ending with
potatoes, layer ingredients in
buttered shallow baking dish.
Pour over all a mixture of:
1 cup veal stock
1 teaspoon salt
1/2 teaspoon white pepper
Bake, covered, in a 375° oven
45 minutes. Remove cover, beat
together and add:
1 cup milk
2 eggs, beaten
Sprinkle with:
1/2 cup bread crumbs
Bake 1/2 hour and serve hot or
cold with yoghurt and sliced
tomatoes.
Serves 4-6

VINETE PRAJITE
Fried Eggplant

Peel, cut into 1/2-inch slices
and sprinkle with salt:
1 large eggplant
Let stand on paper toweling
1 hour, pat dry and dip to coat
slightly in:
flour
In heavy skillet cook for
3 minutes:
4 tablespoons oil or
    rendered pork fat (page 17)
1 leek, minced
Raise heat and brown eggplant
slices until crisp, adding more
oil or fat if needed. Keep cooked
slices hot in slow oven. Season
to taste with:
salt and white pepper
Serve with:
minced parsley
black olives
Good with mixed grill of broiled
pork chops, liver, kidney and
Debabcha (page 102).

VINETE COPT IN UNT
Fried Eggplant in Casserole

In a buttered casserole place
layers of:
Fried Eggplant, preceding recipe
and layers of:
sliced tomatoes

Sprinkle each layer with:
minced parsley
chopped leeks
thyme
white pepper and salt
butter bits
Top with:
more sliced tomatoes,
butter bits and breadcrumbs
Bake in a 375° oven
30 minutes. Garnish with parsley
sprigs and serve as a luncheon
dish with Banitza (page 103).

MAMALIGA DE AUR
Bread of Gold

Follow directions for:
Cornmeal (page 7)
Add just before covering:
1 cup minced mushrooms,
    sautéed, or
1/4 cup crisp bacon bits, or
1/2 cup grated Monterey Jack,
    Cheddar or imported
    Kascaval cheese
butter bits
Layer any one of the above in
a buttered casserole with sliced
cornmeal. Dot with butter, and
bake in a 350° oven until
crisp. Or dip slices in beaten
egg, dredge with grated cheese,
brown both sides, and serve with
yoghurt or sour cream. Good for
breakfast with hot milk or
poached eggs.

NORTHERN EUROPE

THE COLD countries of Northern Europe are densely populated and they exist under the onus of long winter nights and short concentrated growing seasons. Fire and fresh food have always been precious in Ireland, Great Britain, Poland and the Low Countries, even more so in Scandinavia and the northern Soviet Republics. Foods tend to be simpler and plainer than in warmer countries, with rich and poor sharing many common dishes.

Farthest north, where the barbaric Vikings lived, small scattered communities isolated from each other and the rest of the world developed individual special dishes, but with a common pattern. Fertile valleys and pastures were scarce, so enterprising peasants learned to pull cod and herring from the icy seas, pick cloudberries from high mountains, eat wild birds and their eggs, devour reindeer and bear—sometimes raw, with blood still warm—net salmon in rushing streams and gather mushrooms in deep forests. If luck and weather were simultaneously bad, they'd subsist on seaweed, bark, lichen and nettle soup.

The hardy Northmen, faced with the boredom of long nights and scarcity of food, fanned out far and wide by land and sea to plunder, trade and eventually settle in lands less harsh. The flat, warmer areas close-by became battlegrounds where epic struggles have been fought ever since. But what of the people who stayed behind? Also, how did adventurers in tiny fishing vessels dare to venture forth on a mighty ocean? The key to success for both was learning how to cure, salt, pickle, smoke or dry fresh foods when the catch was good and the harvest abundant, thereby spreading feasts through famines or over a long voyage. Salt, used sparingly by early man as a spice, became widely used in large quantities for preserving. Chinese sauerkraut was eagerly adopted from the Mongols, for cabbage grows mightily during the long days of short, cool summers. Today's scientifically bred milk and beef cattle and huge porkers, better homes, factory foods and farm machinery make life easier for many peasant farmers, but old dishes and methods persist.

Flat bread is still made in large cartwheels as it was hundreds of years ago, coming out of the oven limp as linen and almost as unchewable. Only after completely drying out does it attain its crunchy crispness and flavor that last for many months. Less familiar is *gravlax*, a delicious, cured, raw sweet-sour salmon seasoned with mustard, dill, salt and white pepper. S*vartsoppa* (black soup) is a pagan dish of goose and pig's blood now served in more palatable form with the addition of seasonings and wine. Then there's the sour, smelly herring, *surströmming*, prepared by brining, leaving in the hot sun twenty-four hours, then storing at 68° for continued long, slow fermenting. This represents the passive-positive approach to food spoilage peasants so often use. Another example is Danish *øllebrød*, a thick brown soup of stale rye crusts and sweet beer.

Assumed to be of peasant origin, then adopted by the elite in the 18th century is the *smørrebrød*, an open-face sandwich of almost anything on very thin slices of buttered, sour, dark rye bread. Long ago bread slices were used as plates by the aristocracy who deigned to eat only the delicacies served atop them. Peasants were given the juice-laden bread later. After enjoying such flavorful leftovers peasants soon learned how to savor the best of both worlds by eating food and plate together. Aristocrats learned later.

In Norway, cod are salted and spread on cliffs to dry or strung up by the tail to dry slowly in the cold wind for six to twelve weeks, thereby removing over three quarters of the moisture. By then, stiff as boards, they will supposedly keep up to twenty years. To soften for cooking requires soaking in mild lye for two weeks. It was rockbound Norway that spawned the legendary warriors of great strength and courage who fought battles with frenzied rage. From Norway Viking ships embarked for the unknown, provisioned with hard flatbreads, strips of smoked or wind-dried reindeer, salt fish, *fenelar* (thin strips of salted, wind-dried mutton) *smalefötter* (birchwood grilled lamb legs, smoked and wind-dried). While hunger and boredom may have driven some to sunnier shores, it spurred others to dream up unusual foods like *gammelost* (literally, old cheese), a powerful, odoriferous mold-splotched brown cheese made from sour milk. Pickling became an art. Today's pickled salmon is flavored with fresh dill, oil, brandy, pepper, salt and sugar and is served with a sauce of chopped dill, mayonnaise and mustard. Cooks have always tried to outdo each other to relieve the cold monotony of winter, especially in those cooperative cooking contests: wedding feasts.

Sweden, often socially ahead of the times, has recently struck a blow for nostalgia by reviving old peasant dishes like pea soup, salt herring and sour cream, beer-flavored stews, crisp fried pork sausages with pickled beets, cold rose-apple soup, baked beans and back bacon and simmered spiced beef chunks. People there are finding too that the reindeer, which provides the Laplander's entire needs (clothing, shelter and food) is a true delicacy. Herds of reindeer feeding on mushrooms, tender leaves and lichen provide uniquely flavored meat now sold in Scandinavian markets frozen for broiling, roasting or stewing.

Finland shows in its foods the influence of past Swedish and Russian domination. Finnish food tends to be primitive, for Finns feel good things need no tampering. Sauna-cured legs of lamb show a frugal approach. Blood puddings and pancakes, bear meat and whole grain porridge provide the hearty fare one needs at this latitude. Then there's "slaughter soup," chopped meat, heart, liver and kidneys boiled with potatoes and carrots, served with wheat dumplings and barley.

Poland, with mushroom-filled forests, has lived through perennial aggression from its neighbors, yet its people have maintained their early manners and spirit. They're expert at planning ahead for hard winters or hard times by brining all sorts of vegetables and herring, drying fruits or pickling them with cinnamon, cloves and sugar, making jellies and jams and smoked sheep's milk cheese. *Chlodnik*, their cold beet soup, and other similar thick concoctions embellished with dill and sour cream, together with endless homemade pork products, pickled and/or smoked, help revive their indomitable spirits should they lag. In the 14th century a Polish king married to a beautiful Jewess welcomed roving Jews from all over and added their delicious non-pork cuisines to his native pork-based diet. In 1518 King Sigismund's Milanese Queen Bona introduced a number of Italian dishes. Wild game has been so plentiful that *bigos*, or hunter's stew, is considered Poland's most famous dish. Whether this meal-in-a-bowl of cabbage, mushrooms, onions, assorted vegetables, apples and game should be reheated seven times to bring out its best qualities or whether it can be suitably prepared in fresh form by an expert cook is a subject of endless debate.

Russia's vast landscape is characterized by the diversity of its ten cuisines. In classic Russian literature we see their fond preoccupation with food. Vikings, Slavs, Mongols, Turks, Irani, Jews, Gypsies, Chinese Muslims, Indians and Arabs all have contributed swatches of color to Russia's world of foods.

Everyone knows *borsch*, the Russian beet soup, but peasants also make the more common and delicious *shchi* (cabbage) and *jkha* (fish) soups. *Kasha* (coarse cooked buckwheat or other grain) fried in fat then cooked with water in an earthen pot over a low fire is often substituted for scarce meat, especially when perked up with an egg, soup stock or a few meat morsels. Caviar has rarely been available to the poor, but eggplant properly prepared has been called the peasants' substitute. *Bliny*, small wheat, buckwheat, or rye yeast-rising cakes, have been popular for a thousand years, served with melted butter, salted fish and sour cream. These grain-cakes are now served as treats at state dinners. *Blinchiki* are fried twice, then topped with fruit, cheese or meat. *Piroshki* (meat-filled pastries), *pelmeni* (stuffed boiled dumplings) *varenyky* (another boiled dumpling) and Ukranian breads for every occasion demonstrate a few of the endless grain recipes.

Foods of the British Isles, by comparison, sound prosaic, and it's true that many restaurant menus there are unimaginative. Home-prepared dishes are often tastier, and better reflect Britain's varied food heritage. Pre-Roman Celts were uncomplicated eaters. Backed into Ireland, Scotland, Cornwall and Wales—but never subjugated—by successive waves of Angles, Saxons, Jutes, Danes and Normans they stubbornly clung to old foods and customs. England meanwhile became more of a melting pot. While the former Celts would adopt only an occasional food, like the American potato, the English took advantage of more sophisticated continental cooking including the Norman's fancy breads and pastry, tripe with onions, dishes cooked in wine and beer. Originally only herbs were used for seasoning, later salt and pepper, finally cinnamon, nutmeg, cloves and ginger. Until 1700, when turnips were found to be good fodder, there was little to keep the scrawny cattle, pigs and sheep alive during cold, damp winters. Most were slaughtered and salted in late autumn. Their meat was tough and tasteless; if not quickly salted, it often became tainted. Herbs, spices and strong sauces were needed to make it palatable. Gradually breeds were improved, transportation became more efficient, and fresh meat without heavy seasoning became a staple. Today good, fresh ingredients—meat, game, vegetables and fruit—unsauced and unsubtle, are a hallmark of British food, though some feel that meat has been overbred on the bland side and there is a longing for the older, stronger flavors. Bacon and ham are exceptions. These English inventions from the dim past have not only survived but have spread around the world—(in the old days "bacon" denoted fresh pork in the rest of Europe). Other old dishes have not taken the world by storm, but remain local specialties. Eaten with hot milk, *frumenty* is prepared by soaking wheat or barley in warmed water for several days. The grains slowly swell and finally burst, forming a healthful thick starchy suspension of ruptured hulls. Welsh *oatcakes* in buttermilk and *oatmeal broth* show none of the Norman influence, nor do the Scottish baking powder *scones*,

Cornish miners' lunch *pasties* with meat filling, or Ireland's *soda bread* cooked in a peat fire. Traditionally everyone ate hearty breakfasts of home-grown farm food or local fish; but agriculture is on the wane, and factory foods amounting to lighter meals are growing more popular. No one really believes, however, there'll be an end to homemade steamed puddings that so pleasantly fill and warm the stomach on a nasty night (and are easy on poor teeth so common in Great Britain). *Haggis*, first known in Ireland and England, but popularly assumed to be the national dish of the frugal Scots, utilizes the offal left after a sheep's pelt is used for a warm jacket and its mutton is roasted or salted away. The offal is boiled, then chopped and mixed with suet, oats or barley and dried herbs to be stuffed into the sheep's stomach and boiled some more. The finished product keeps for days like a large sausage, though some claim it can get extremely ripe before being rejected by a true Scotsman. Fish and chips (bought at a stand, wrapped in newspaper and dressed on the spot with salt and malt vinegar) must be considered British peasant food just as much as porridge, Yorkshire pudding or home potted, pickled or jellied fish or meat.

Benelux may stand for the commercial banding together of three tiny countries—Belgium, Netherlands, and Luxembourg—but they are far from homogeneous in terms of food styles. Flemish, Dutch, French, Catholic, Protestant, even Spanish influences color local approaches to food; borrowing ideas is common, though seldom admitted. Peasants here live close to the sea, many below sea level, and they especially savor eels, oysters, shrimp, crab and all kinds of fish. So much of the food is locally produced that freshness adds an extra filip to its flavor. Endive, Brussels sprouts, and other vegetables are picked and consumed at their prime. Lightly salted whole herring are eaten out of hand like hot dogs, tasting delicately raw. Fresh vegetables are added to green split-pea soup to make it even greener, while pigs' feet, slices of sausage, and savory contribute body and flavor. Famous Flemish *waterzooi*, a vegetable-base soup, makes a full meal with its large chunks of chicken or fish.

It's been said that the countries of Northern Europe have either an arctic climate or no climate at all—just lots of weather. In any case, the cold countries have evolved food styles which combine simplicity and vitality.

SJÖMANSBIFF
Sailor's Beef

Sauté in:
2 tablespoons butter
**1-1/2 pounds beef round, thinly
    sliced and pounded**
2 onions, sliced
Layer in shallow buttered
baking dish:
meat slices
onions
**5 potatoes, peeled and
    thickly sliced**
Sprinkle each layer with:
salt and white pepper
End layering with potato.
Deglaze (page 17) frying pan
with:
1 cup hot beef stock or water
Add:
1 cup dark beer
Pour liquid over meat and
potatoes. Cover and cook in
a 375° oven 1-1/2 hours
until tender. Sprinkle with
plenty of:
minced parsley
Serve with buttered carrots
or pickled beets (page 162).
Serves 6

FASAN
Pheasant

Sprinkle with:
salt and pepper
large pheasant, cut up
Brown on all sides in:
2 tablespoons bacon drippings
Butter and line a shallow
earthenware baking dish with:
2 unpared apples, sliced
**I large orange, skinned
    and sliced**
1/2 cup pitted, halved prunes
Place pheasant pieces on top.
Deglaze (page 17) browning
pan with:
**3/4 cup each water and
    dry white wine**
Pour over pheasant.
Cover tightly and bake in
a 350° oven 1 hour or until
tender. Serve with browned whole
new potatoes and fresh spinach,
watercress or lettuce salad.
Serves 4

SWEDEN

STEKT KYCKLING
Roast Chicken

Sprinkle inside and out with:
salt and white pepper
1 4-pound roasting chicken
In cavity put:
1 large bunch parsley
Rub skin well with:
3 tablespoons softened butter
In Dutch oven brown on all
sides in a 450° oven. Add:
3/4 cup hot chicken stock
Cover and cook, basting
occasionally, in a 350° oven
1 hour or until tender. Remove to
heated serving platter and keep
warm. Reduce liquid in Dutch oven
by half. Then add:
1/2 cup cream
Heat (do not boil) and pour over
chicken. Serve with green salad
and boiled or mashed potatoes.
Serves 6

INLAGD SILL
Pickled Salt Herring

Soak overnight in cold water
or milk:
1 pound salt herring
If very salty, soak in several
changes of water or milk 3 or 4
hours longer. Discard skin and
small bones, rinse and drain.
Cut crosswise into thin slices.
Follow directions for **Pickled
Smelts** (page 112). Arrange
drained herring on platter and
garnish attractively with onion
rings, fresh minced chives or dill,
and parsley sprigs. May be made
ahead of time.
Serves 6-8

PLÄTTAR
Dessert Pancakes

Add to crêpe batter (page 13):
2 teaspoons sugar
In a plättpanna, (special pan for
frying Swedish crêpes;
substitute any 7-8-inch skillet),
cook as directed and serve with:
lingonberries
cranberries, or
any jam or fruit

SAFFRANSBROD
Saffron Bread

This bread is in every Swedish
house at Christmas.

Prepare batter for:
**Basic Sweet Bread Dough
   (page 8)**
and add:
1/4 teaspoon saffron
1/2 cup chopped raisins
After first rising, divide dough
in half. Shape each half into
braids by rolling the dough
3/4-inch thick and then cutting
it into 8-inch strips and
shaping these into round strands.
Twist into desired shapes.
Decorate with:
raisins
Brush with:
beaten egg
Bake in 350° oven 25 minutes.
Cover and cool on rack. Good
served with jam and/or relishes.

GROLANGKAALSUPPE
Hearty Winter Kale Soup

Blanch (page 17) 5 minutes,
drain and dice:
1/2 pound salt pork
Combine with:
2 quarts water
1 pound kale, chopped
1 onion, chopped
2 leeks, chopped
**2 cups each diced potatoes
   and carrots**
Bring to boil, cover and simmer
1-1/2 hours. Season to taste with:
salt and black pepper
In Denmark this soup is made with
a greater quantity of salt pork
(2-3 pounds) which is sliced and
eaten with mustard and dark bread
along with the soup. May be
made ahead of time.
Serves 8

LEVERPOSTEJ
Liver Pâté

Grind finely:
1-1/2 pounds pork liver, cut up
1/2 pound pork fat, cut up
1 onion
1/4 cup parsley
**2 canned anchovy fillets
   (optional)**
In a saucepan melt:
4 tablespoons butter
Sprinkle with:
3 tablespoons flour
Cook and stir 3 minutes and
gradually add:
1 cup milk
Cook and stir until smooth and
thickened and add:
1 teaspoon salt
1/2 teaspoon allspice
1/4 teaspoon black pepper
2 tablespoons sherry
Combine with liver mixture, pour
into a 9x5 loaf pan, set the pan
in a pan of water and bake in
a 350° oven 1 hour. Chill
before slicing. May be made
ahead of time.
Serves 10

FRIKADELLE
Fried Meatballs

Combine:
**1/2 pound each ground pork
   and veal**
**1 medium onion, grated finely
   to release juices**
1 egg, beaten
1/2 cup milk
3 tablespoons flour
1 teaspoon salt
1/4 teaspoon white pepper
Form mixture into small balls
and sauté until browned on
all sides in:
**half bacon drippings and
   half butter**
Remove to heated platter and
keep warm. Sprinkle skillet with:
1 tablespoon flour
Cook and stir 3 minutes, and
gradually add:
1/2 cup stock
Cook and stir until thickened
and smooth. Season to taste with:
salt and white pepper
Pour over meatballs. Serve with
mashed potatoes and creamed
peas and carrots or cranberries.
Serves 4

DENMARK/NORWAY

RABABER GROD
Rhubarb

Combine:
**1 quart rhubarb, cut in 1-inch
   lengths**
3/4 cup sugar
1-1/2 cups water
Bring to boil and simmer
5 minutes or until fruit is
softened.
Thicken with a mixture of:
**2 tablespoons potato starch
   dissolved in**
2 tablespoons water
Cool, chill and serve with cold
milk. Can also be made with half
rhubarb and half strawberries,
gooseberries, or red and black
currants and raspberries.
May be made ahead of time.
Serves 6

AVKOKT TORSK
Norwegian Poached Cod

Bring to boil:
**enough Court Bouillon
   to cover (page 16)**
6 1-inch thick cod steaks
Lower heat to medium, add steaks
and poach gently 5 minutes or
until tender. Remove to heated
platter and pour over steaks:
6 tablespoons melted butter
3 tablespoons lemon juice
2 tablespoons minced parsley
Serve with hot mustard and
a creamed vegetable; may also be
served with cucumber slices
dredged in flour, salt, pepper
and dill and browned in butter.
To serve cold, omit melted
butter and garnish with sour
cream, dill and sliced raw
cucumbers.
Serves 6

DESSERT CHEESES

Sweden: Bergquara, Hable
           Crème Chantilly

Denmark: Danablu (especially
           good with apples),
           Crema Danica (with
           black cherries)
           Cabrinnet

Norway: Taffelsot

ZUPA SZCZAWIOWA
Sorrel Soup

Bring to boil:
2 quarts strong beef stock
Add:
1 pound each sorrel and
**   spinach leaves, coarsely**
**   chopped**
1 pound potatoes, peeled
**   and diced**
2 onions, diced
1 teaspoon each salt and sugar
Bring back to boil, cover and
simmer 30 minutes. Serve with
Peasant Bread (page 8).
May be made ahead of time.
Serves 8

SALAD IDEAS

Serve sliced cucumbers or
beets in a dill-vinegar
dressing, or in sour cream.
Dress sliced tomatoes to taste
with vinegar, salt, oil,
chives, chopped cucumbers,
minced onion, dill or
combinations.
Mix grated carrots with
grated apples, horseradish,
sour cream, sugar, parsley,
salt to taste; serve as
side dish.

BIGOS
Mixed Stew

Sprinkle with:
2 tablespoons salt
1 quart shredded cabbage
Mix well and let stand 2 hours.
Rinse and drain, press out all
the moisture and set aside.

Sauté until crisp:
4 strips bacon, diced
Remove with slotted spoon and
reserve.
In bacon drippings sauté the
drained cabbage 3 minutes then
remove to large kettle.
Sauté until soft, adding
more drippings if needed:
2 large onions, diced
2 large cooking apples,
**   pared and diced**
1/4 pound fresh mushrooms,
**   sliced**
Transfer these to kettle with
cabbage and brown in fat:
2 pounds venison or any
**   combination of lamb, veal, pork**
**   or beef, cut into 1-inch cubes**
Add to kettle with:
1 cup each stock and
**   dry red wine**
1/4 cup tomato purée
6 peppercorns
1 teaspoon salt

Bring to boil, cover and simmer
1 hour or until meat is almost
tender. Then add:
1/2 Polish sausage, sliced
Cook 1/2 hour longer and serve
sprinkled with reserved bacon
bits. May be made ahead of time.
Serves 8

PIERNIK
Honey Cake Traditionally
Served on Rosh Hashanah

Sift together:
3 cups sifted unbleached flour
2 teaspoons baking powder
1 teaspoon each baking soda
**   and cinnamon**
1/2 teaspoon nutmeg
1/4 teaspoon each salt
**   and ginger**
1/8 teaspoon ground cloves
Beat until thick and frothy:
4 eggs
Gradually add:
1 cup each sugar and dark honey
1/4 cup salad oil
Blend into flour mixture
alternately with:
3/4 cup strong black coffee
Fold in:
1 cup ground walnuts
Pour into greased 9-inch tube
pan and bake in a 325° oven
50-60 minutes or until
tests done.

RUSSIA

SHAV
Spinach Borsht

Bring to boil:
6 cups water
Add and boil 5 minutes:
**1 pound spinach, coarsely
   chopped**
Beat:
4 eggs
1 teaspoon salt
Whisk into 2 cups of hot soup
and beat into rest of soup.
Do not allow to boil. Adjust
seasonings with:
salt and pepper
Cool. Serve with sour cream
and Vatrushky.
Serves 4

VATRUSHKY
Cheese Tarts

Make:
**1 recipe Cream Cheese Pastry
   (page 13)**
Set aside.
Combine:
12 ounces cream cheese
6 tablespoons sour cream
2 teaspoons sugar
1/2 teaspoon salt
**1/2 teaspoon freshly grated
   lemon peel**
1/2 cup currants
Roll pastry 1/8 inch thick, cut
into 3-inch rounds and press
into small muffin tins. Fill
with cheese mixture and bake in
a 375° oven 15 minutes or
until edges are golden.
Makes 24

SHCHI
Cabbage Soup

Cook until limp:
1/4 pound slab bacon, diced
Sprinkle with:
1 tablespoon flour
Cook and stir to brown and add:
2 quarts beef stock.
Stir to blend flour and add:
3 carrots, diced
2 onions, diced
**1 cup each diced potatoes and
   turnips**
1/2 cup diced celery and tops
3 tomatoes, chopped
1/3 cup minced parsley
1 small cabbage, chopped
Bring to boil and simmer 1 hour.
Serve with:
sour cream
Sprinkle with:
dill weed
Pass a bowl of Kasha.
Serves 6

KASHA
Buckwheat (Groats)

Combine:
1 cup whole grain buckwheat
1 egg, beaten
Let stand 10 minutes. Heat iron
skillet and over medium heat fry
the kasha, stirring constantly,
until dry and slightly browned.
Then add:
2 cups boiling water or stock
Cover and simmer 20 minutes until
tender.
Sauté in:
2 tablespoons butter or
rendered chicken fat (page 17)
3/4 cup chopped onion
Add to Kasha and mix well.
Serve as side dish with soup,
meat or poultry.
Serves 6

KASHA VARNISHKAS

Omit onions from Kasha recipe
and add:
2 tablespoons softened butter
or rendered chicken fat
(page 17)
2-1/2 cups cooked bowtie
macaroni

VINYEGRYET
Salad Vinaigrette

Combine:
1/2 cup diced cooked beets
1 cup each cooked peas
and diced carrots
1 large apple, unpeeled
and diced
1 cup diced cooked potatoes
4 green onions, thinly sliced
salt, black pepper and
paprika to taste

Make a paste of:
1 tablespoon Russian Mustard
(following recipe)
2 tablespoons oil
1 tablespoon sugar
Mix into paste:
2 tablespon oil
Pour over vegetables and
marinate overnight, stirring
occasionally. One hour before
serving mix in:
1/4 cup sour cream
Arrange vegetables on lettuce
leaves and sprinkle with:
minced parsley
Garnish with:
chopped hard-cooked eggs
Serve with Piroshki (page 112).
Serves 6

RUSSIAN MUSTARD

Combine:
1/2 cup dry mustard
1 cup sugar
1/4 teaspoon salt
Pour over, stirring constantly:
3/4 cup boiling water
Blend to make a paste, adding
more water if needed. Then add:
1 teaspoon white vinegar
1 tablespoon salad oil
Adjust seasonings to taste and
store in refrigerator.

RUSSIA

PIROSHKI
Meat Pastries

Make 1 recipe of:
Cream Cheese Pastry (page 13)
Simmer until no longer pink:
1/2 pound ground round steak
1 tablespoon water
Add:
1 tablespoon flour
1/2 teaspoon salt
**1/4 teaspoon each black pepper,
    paprika and thyme**
Sauté until soft in:
1 tablespoon butter
1/3 cup minced onion
1 garlic clove, finely minced
Combine with meat mixture and:
2 hard-cooked eggs, chopped
Adjust seasonings and cool. Roll
pastry 1/8-inch thick and cut
into 3-inch rounds. Place
a teaspoon of filling on each,
fold over into half-moon shape,
seal and place, seam side **up**,
on baking sheet. Bake in a 375°
oven 10 minutes or until golden.
Can be frozen before baking.
Serve with soup and/or salad.
Makes 24

PIROG
Fish in Pastry

Cook and set aside:
**3/4 cup raw rice (1-1/2 cups
    cooked)**
Make double recipe of:
Cream Cheese Pastry (page 13)
Rub into:
**1 pound firm boneless white fish
    cut into 3/4-inch cubes**
1 teaspoon salt, mixed with
**1/2 teaspoon each black pepper
    and thyme**
Let stand 2 hours.

Sauté until soft in:
2 tablespoons butter
1 cup minced onions
**1/2 cup minced fresh or
    softened dried mushrooms**

Remove with slotted spatula and
brown fish cubes on all sides,
adding more butter as needed.
Do not overcook.
Cool and add:
reserved onions and mushrooms
1/4 cup minced parsley
**1/2 teaspoon crushed
    fennel seeds or**
**3 tablespoons chopped
    fresh chervil**
the cooked rice
2 hard-cooked eggs, chopped
Stir with fork to just mix,
adjust seasonings to taste and
set aside. Roll pastry 1/4-inch
thick into 2 ovals. Divide
filling on each, bring edges
up and around, seal with a
little water and place on cookie
sheet, seam side down. Form
into shape of fish and decorate
with pastry scraps to make
eyes, fins and tail. Prick
with tines of fork in pattern
down each side and bake in
a 375° oven 30 minutes
until golden.
Serves 6

SNYETKI V MARINADYE
Pickled Smelts

Sprinkle with:
salt and pepper
1 pound bait-size smelts
Fry in hot oil 2 minutes per
side; do not overcook.
Transfer to shallow dish.
In saucepan bring to boil and
boil 1 minute:
1 cup white vinegar
1 Bermuda onion, sliced
10 peppercorns
2 whole cloves
1 bay leaf
Remove from heat and cool.
Pour over fish and refrigerate
at least 12 hours. Serve as
an appetizer or as a main dish
with dilled boiled potatoes.
May be made ahead of time.
Serves 4-6

PELMENI
Meat-Filled Dumplings

Prepare batter for:
Chinese noodle dough (page 13)
Add while sifting:
1 teaspoon sugar
If using ready-made wonton
skins, add sugar to filling.
For the filling, sauté until
golden in:
1 tablespoon butter
1/2 cup finely minced onion
Add and cook uncovered until
meat loses color:
12 ounces lean ground beef, or
half beef and half pork
Season to taste with:
salt and pepper
Set aside to cool.

Roll dough into 48 rounds or
squares. Place about 3/4 teaspoon
of filling on each, fold over and
seal, using water if needed. As
they are formed cover with a tea
towel to prevent drying out.
Bring to boil:
6 cups rich stock
Reduce heat slightly and cook
the pelmeni 10 or so at a time
until they rise to surface.
Do not overcook.
Remove with slotted spoon
and keep warm.
When all are cooked drizzle
over them:
4 tablespoons melted butter
2 tablespoons of the stock
Garnish with dill and serve
with sour cream.
Serves 4-6

RUSSIA

LOX
Salted Salmon

Prepare by the following
method:
1 whole salmon
Remove head and fins, scale
and cut in half lengthwise (do
not wash). Rub all surfaces
evenly with a mixture of:
1/2 cup coarse salt
4 teaspoons sugar
20 white peppercorns
This quantity is for 4 pounds
prepared salmon; if fish is
smaller, use proportionately
less of mixture.
Place one-half of salmon, skin
side down, on large platter.
Place a second piece, skin side
up, on top so the thicker end
meets the thinner end. Cover
with plastic wrap and place
a weight on top to draw out
excess moisture. Let stand
in a cool place (not in the
refrigerator) 24 hours. Scrape
salt mixture off and wipe well
with paper toweling. To serve,
slice slantwise across grain,
discarding skin. To store up to
1 week, wrap well and
refrigerate. Serve with Bagels
(page 6) and cream cheese,
or with new potatoes.

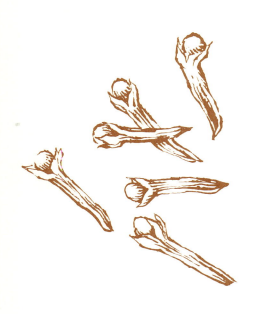

ORYEKHOVYI SOUS
Chicken with Walnut Sauce

Dredge in:
flour, salt and pepper
1 3-pound chicken, cut up
Sauté until golden in:
3 tablespoons oil
1 garlic clove
Discard garlic and brown chicken
on all sides.

Cover and cook over medium
heat 20-30 minutes or until
tender. Remove to heated platter
and keep warm.
In same skillet melt:
2 tablespoons butter or rendered
chicken fat (page 17)
Add:
1 garlic clove, minced
1/2 cup each chopped walnuts
and onion
Stir and cook until onions are
transparent. Then sprinkle with:
1 tablespoon flour
Cook and stir 3 minutes. Add:
1 cup chicken stock
1/8 teaspoon each allspice,
nutmeg and cinnamon
1 tablespoon vinegar
salt and pepper to taste
Cook and stir until smooth and
slightly thickened, pour over
chicken and sprinkle liberally
with minced parsley. Serve with
Kasha Varnishkas (page 111).
Serves 4-6

PUTCHAH
Calf's Feet Broth or Jelly

**Jelly traditionally served
at Jewish weddings**

Combine, bring to boil, cover
and simmer 2 hours:
6 cups water
**2 calf's feet, cut into
    4 sections, blanched (page 17)
    5 minutes and rinsed**
1 whole carrot
1 whole peeled onion
1/2 cup celery leaves
2 parsley roots*
6 peppercorns
1 bay leaf
2 whole garlic cloves
1 teaspoon salt
Strain, remove meat from bones,
mince finely and reserve. Cool
the broth (which will have cooked
down to about 3 cups), refrigerate
and defat. Combine and heat
to boiling:
the defatted broth
1 cup water
reserved meat
Beat together:
3 eggs
**1/4 cup each lemon juice and
    sugar**

Whisk into 1 cup of hot broth,
return to rest of broth and
stir to thicken but do not boil.
Serve with Challah (page 8).

To serve as jelly:
If chilled broth is too
gelatinous, heat with water
and cool, reserving 1 cup.
Add reserved meat and
pour into a 9x13-inch shallow
serving dish. Let set slightly,
top with sliced hard-cooked
eggs to make an over-all pattern,
carefully pour reserved broth
over and chill until set. To
serve cut into squares. Very
gelatinous and rich.
Serve also with Challah (page 8).
Serves 6-8

BLINTZES
Crêpe Dessert

Add to:
1 recipe crêpe batter (page 13)
2 teaspoons sugar
Cook as directed and fill with
one of the following fillings.

1 pound dry cottage cheese
1 egg, beaten
1 tablespoon sugar
1/2 teaspoon cinnamon
1/4 teaspoon salt
1/3 cup raisins (optional)

**1-1/2 cups cooked blueberries
    or cherries**
**1-1/2 tablespoons each sugar
    and flour**
**1/8 teaspoon each cinnamon
    and nutmeg**

2 cups pared, diced apple
1-1/2 tablespoons ground almonds
1 tablespoon sugar
1/8 teaspoon cinnamon
2 tablespoons lemon juice
Roll and place in lightly
buttered shallow baking dish.
Bake in a 300° oven
15 minutes and serve with
sour cream.
Serves 6

ENGLAND

FISH AND CHIPS

For the chips, peel and cut
into 3/4-inch finger-length
slices:
2 pounds potatoes
Place in cold water 10 minutes,
drain and dry thoroughly. Fry
in 400° deep fat until
golden, drain on paper toweling,
salt and keep warm in low oven.
Combine and beat until smooth:
1 cup sifted unbleached flour
3/4 cup milk
1 egg
2 tablespoons water
Cut in half lengthwise:
3 pounds firm white fish filets
    (flounder, sole, perch,
    halibut, etc.)
Dust fish with:
flour, salt and pepper
Dip in batter and fry in 400°
deep fat until golden. Drain
on paper toweling and serve
immediately with salt, malt
vinegar and the potatoes.
Serves 6-8

KIDNEY AND SAUSAGE PIE

Remove suet from:
1 pound beef or veal kidneys
Mince enough of the suet to
make 1 tablespoon. Cut the
kidneys into 1-inch cubes,
blanch (page 17) 2 minutes,
drain and dust with:
2 tablespoons flour
Sauté kidneys in the suet with:
2 tablespoons flour
Sauté kidneys in the suet with:
1/2 pound Sage Sausage
    (page 117)
1/2 cup each chopped onion and
    celery with some tops
Stir well and add:
1 cup thinly sliced carrots
1/2 cup water
1/4 cup dry sherry
1/2 teaspoon salt
1/4 teaspoon black pepper
1/8 teaspoon cayenne pepper
Bring to gentle boil, cover
and simmer 20 minutes. Transfer
to deep 9-inch casserole and top
with:
Biscuit Pastry Dough (page 13)
Bake in a 425° oven
35 minutes until top is golden.
Serves 4

CORNISH PASTIES
Meat-Vegetable Pies

Prepare 1 recipe:
Hot Water Pastry (page 13)
For filling combine:
1-1/2 cups diced beef
    round steak
1 cup diced potato
1/2 cup each diced onion
    and turnip
1/4 cup chopped parsley
1 teaspoon salt
1/2 teaspoon black pepper
3 tablespoons finely
    minced suet
2 tablespoons water
Roll pastry 1/4-inch thick, cut
into 14 6-inch rounds and place
1/4 cup filling on each. Fold
over and seal edges with tines
of fork. Prick in several places
and brush with a mixture of:
water and beaten egg
Bake in a 400° oven 10 minutes.
Lower heat to 350° and bake
25 minutes more. Serve hot or
at room temperature.
Makes 14

SHEPHERD'S PIE

Combine and place in buttered
1-1/2-quart baking dish:
2 cups leftover meat, minced
   or ground
1/2 cup finely minced onion
2/3 cup leftover meat gravy
   (or brown sauce)
1/4 cup minced parsley
1/4 cup finely minced celery
1/4 teaspoon sage
salt and pepper to taste
Cover with:
2 cups mashed potatoes, softened
   with milk if necessary
Dot with:
4 tablespoons butter bits
1/4 cup grated cheese (optional)
Bake in a 400° oven
15 minutes to heat through and
brown top. Try variations with
any combination of meats, vegetables, sautéed mushrooms, etc.
Serves 4-6

BANBURY TARTS
Raisin Tarts

Make 1 recipe:
Hot Water Pastry (page 13)
Combine:
1 cup chopped raisins
2/3 cup sugar
1 egg, beaten
2 tablespoons crushed
   soda crackers
1 teaspoon freshly grated
   lemon rind
3 tablespoons lemon juice
Roll pastry 1/8-inch thick, cut
into 3-inch rounds and place
1 teaspoon filling on each
round. Fold round over to form
half-moon shape, seal with tines
of fork and place on baking
sheet. Bake in a 375° oven
20 minutes or until golden. Can
be frozen before or after baking.
Makes 40-48

BRANDY GINGER BALLS

Cream together:
1/2 pound butter
1/2 cup each brown sugar
   and molasses
2 tablespoons brandy, sherry
   or orange juice
Sift and add to above:
2 cups unbleached flour
1-1/2 teaspoons powdered ginger
1/2 teaspoon each nutmeg
   and salt
Mix well and form into walnut-
size balls. Place on greased
cookie sheet and bake in a
300° oven 15 minutes.
Remove while warm, sift:
powdered sugar
over all. When cool sift over
more powdered sugar. Store
in cool place.
Makes 48

SCOTLAND

SCOTTISH EGGS

Prepare following recipe for,
but do not cook:
Sage Sausage
Roll out sausage meat and encase
it around:
6 hard-cooked eggs
Dip coated eggs in:
beaten egg
bread crumbs
Fry in hot deep fat until golden.
Drain on paper toweling, halve
and serve hot or cold.

SAGE SAUSAGE

Combine and refrigerate
overnight to blend flavors:
1 pound ground lean pork
1 teaspoon salt
1 tablespoon each sage and
  marjoram
1/4 teaspoon black pepper
1/8 teaspoon each cayenne
  pepper and powdered cloves
Use as directed in Scottish
Eggs or Kidney and Sausage Pie
(page 115).
Or form into patties and sauté
slowly to brown both sides and
cook meat thoroughly. Serve
with poached eggs and/or
boiled potatoes.
Serves 4-6

SHORTBREAD

Cream together:
1/2 pound butter, softened
1/2 cup light brown sugar
1 teaspoon almond extract
  (optional)

Sift together:
2 cups sifted unbleached flour
1/4 teaspoon each salt and
  baking powder
Blend into butter mixture, place
on cookie sheet and pat into
a rectangle 1/4-inch thick,
using as little flour as
possible. Make cut marks to
outline 1-1/2-inch squares and
prick each square with tines of
fork. Bake in a 350° oven
15-20 minutes until light and
golden. Do not overcook. Remove
to cake rack in individual
squares, cool and store in tin
with tight lid.
Makes 4 dozen

COUNTRY SOUP
Great after a country outing

Bring to boil:
3 quarts water
2 pounds lamb neck bones,
    leftover leg and scraps,
    or other bones
2 bay leaves
2 teaspoons salt
Cover and simmer 1-1/2 hours.
Strain, dice and reserve meat;
then add to stock:
1 cup each lentils and
    split peas
3 carrots, diced
2 leeks and some tops, chopped
1/2 medium cabbage, shredded
1 teaspoon salt
1/2 teaspoon black pepper
1/4 teaspoon thyme
Bring to boil and simmer 1 hour
or until vegetables are tender.
Return meat to pot, reheat
and serve with Irish Soda Bread.
Serves 10-12

IRISH SODA BREAD

Sift together:
2 cups sifted unbleached flour
1 teaspoon baking soda
1/2 teaspoon salt
Cut in until crumbly:
2 tablespoons butter

Combine:
1/4 cup white vinegar
1/2 cup milk
Add to flour mixture and
blend well. Then stir in:
3 tablespoons currants
Turn out on floured board and
knead briefly until smooth. Pat
into a well-buttered 9-inch
round cake pan. Bake in a 375°
oven 25 minutes. Cut into wedges
and serve hot with butter.

IRISH STEW

Scald and rinse:
1 pound marrow bones, sawed
    into 1-inch pieces
2 pounds lamb or mutton shoulder,
    cut into pieces
Arrange in heavy kettle and
place on top in alternate layers:
2-3 onions, sliced
6 boiling potatoes, thickly
    sliced
Sprinkle layers with:
1 teaspoon salt
1/2 teaspoon black pepper
1/4 teaspoon thyme
Add water to almost cover top
layer, bring to boil, cover
and simmer 1 hour or until meat
is tender. Remove marrow bones
and serve the marrow in separate
dish to be spread on bread.
Serves 4

FARMER FRUIT CAKE

Bring to boil:
1 cup water, stout or coffee
1/2 cup each sugar, sultanas,
    currants and candied fruit
1/4 pound butter
Cool to lukewarm.
Sift together and add:
2 cups unbleached whole-wheat
    pastry flour
1-1/2 teaspoons baking soda
1/2 teaspoon each salt,
    allspice and cinnamon
1/4 teaspoon nutmeg
Add:
1/2 cup chopped nut meats
    (optional)
Pour into greased 9-inch square
pan lined with wax paper and
bake in a 350° oven 30-40
minutes.
Serve warm or cool. If desired,
pour dry sherry over cake and
store 2 days before cutting.
Good, quick and easy.

BELGIUM

JAMBON ET CHICORÉE
Ham and Endive Rolls

Bring to boil:
2 cups water
1 tablespoon sugar
Dip into the boiling water for
2 minutes and drain thoroughly:
4 medium endive, trimmed**
and washed
Wrap around each:
2 thin slices baked ham
Place rolls in buttered baking
dish in one layer. Then add:
1/2 cup stock or water
Dot each roll with:
2 teaspoons butter bits
Sprinkle the rolls with:
2 tablespoons bread crumbs
1 cup grated Gouda cheese
Bake in a 350° oven
30 minutes until heated and
cheese is melted.
Serves 4

**What we call French endive.
Can vary recipe with leeks or
quartered iceberg lettuce.

CARBONNADES FLAMANDES
Beef Casserole

Season with:
salt and pepper
1-1/2 pounds chuck or rump beef
cut into small cubes
Brown beef quickly in:
2 tablespoons rendered beef
fat and/or butter
Transfer to casserole.
Adding more fat if needed, sauté
until golden:
1-1/2 cups chopped onion
Sprinkle with:
1-1/2 tablespoons flour
Cook and stir 3 minutes,
then add:
1-1/2 cups dark beer (or
water or stock)
Cook and stir until smooth and
pour over casserole with:
1 garlic clove, finely minced
1 bay leaf
1/4 cup minced parsley
Bring to boil, cover and cook
in a 375° oven 1-1/2 hours
or until meat is tender,
checking occasionally for
moisture. Adjust to taste with:
salt and pepper
Just before serving add:
2 teaspoons vinegar
Serve with plain boiled potatoes.
Serves 4

ASPERGES
Asparagus

Steam until tender-crisp:
fresh asparagus
Serve each portion with a
mixture of:
1 soft-boiled egg
salt and pepper
minced parsley
melted butter
lemon juice

MOULES ET FRITES
Mussels and Fried Potatoes

Serve steamed clams or mussels
with fried potatoes
(see Fish and Chips, page 115)
that have been fried in:
half fat and half lard
Popular all over Belgium and
sold from pushcarts.

WITLOOF
Belgian Endive

Toss endive with oil and
vinegar to taste and garnish
with thinly sliced sweet red
pepper; eat plain with salt; or
dress with a vinaigrette
dressing.

HAZEPEPER MET ZUURKOOL
Rabbit with Sauerkraut

Dust lightly in:
salt and pepper
2 tablespoons flour
**1 rabbit or hare, cut into
    serving pieces**
Brown on all sides in:
butter
Add:
1 onion, chopped
1 cup stock
**1/2 teaspoon each paprika
    and nutmeg**
1 bay leaf
2 cups well-washed sauerkraut
Bring to gentle boil, cover
and simmer 1 hour or until
rabbit is tender. Serve
with boiled or mashed potatoes.
Serves 4-6

BRUINE BONEN SOEP
Brown Bean Soup

Soak overnight, rinse and drain:
1 cup brown beans
Combine with:
3 quarts water
1 bay leaf
**2 tablespoons bacon or
    ham drippings**
1/2 teaspoon black pepper
1/4 teaspoon nutmeg

Bring to gentle boil, cover
and simmer 2 hours or until
beans are tender but still
retain their shape.
Sauté in:
2 tablespoons butter
1 onion, chopped
Add last 15 minutes
to soup with:
**1 bratwurst, sliced on
    diagonal 1/4-inch thick**
Sprinkle with minced parsley
and serve with Potato Bread
(page 10).
Serves 6-8

VISCHKOEKJES
Fish Cakes

Soak in:
1 cup milk
2 slices bread

Combine soaked bread with:
3 cups cooked fish, flaked
1 egg, beaten
1/4 cup chopped parsley
1/2 teaspoon salt
**1/4 teaspoon each black pepper
    and nutmeg**
Form into 3-inch cakes and brown
on both sides in:
**3 tablespoons each butter
    and oil**
Makes 12 3-inch cakes

APPELKOEK
Apple Cake

Cream together:
1/4 pound softened butter
1 cup brown sugar
Add and mix in:
2 eggs
1 teaspoon vanilla

Sift together:
2 cups unbleached flour
1 teaspoon baking soda
1/2 teaspoon salt
Add flour to butter mixture
    alternately with:
1/3 cup orange juice
Blend in:
**1 teaspoon freshly grated
    orange peel**
1/2 cup chopped walnuts
1 cup pared, chopped apples
Pour into greased 5x9 loaf
pan and bake 1 hour in
a 350° oven. Serve with
cream cheese.

WEST INDIES

THE APPEAL of calypso music lies in its happy absurdity. To exaggerated syncopated rhythm, outlandish characters like the "Great Lord Wonder" shout gossipy, spicy ballads, each impromptu or original. No true calypso singer would ever sing another's songs. Calypso's black humor dates back to colonial times when slaves toiling in the Caribbean cane fields needed an antidote for despair. Their harsh masters forbade conversation, so they gossiped in song. By adding laments, and stories of love and protest, too, the ebullient slaves turned ancestral jungle rhythms into exciting music. Similarly, the bland African foods they had brought with them, *okra*, *taro* and *akee*, were turned into zesty Caribbean dishes by adding imaginative blends of local fruits, vegetables, herbs, spices and—most important—hot peppers of great variety. *Okra* cooked with *funchi* (cornmeal pudding) became *coo-coo*. With mashed *plantains* (over-size, unsweet bananas) it became *foo-foo*. "Elephant ears," the spinach-like leaves of *taro* were an essential component of *callaloo*, a thick spicy soup. Starchy taro roots were eaten like potatoes. To be appreciated, the peach-sized *akee* had to be cooked as a vegetable like many another tropical fruit. Its only edible parts, large *ariles* (seed appendages), have a scrambled-egg flavor, which in a casserole contrasts well with salt fish, onions and peppers.

It's easy to see why Columbus the dreamer thought he'd found the Garden of Eden as he explored the Caribbean. Here thousands of tropical islands arch from Florida to eastern Venezuela, some with lush vegetation, some rocky, all made pleasant by southeast trade winds. Luckily—for him, for Spain and for the European world—Columbus received a friendly welcome from the gentle Arawak natives and even at first from the local cannibals, the Caribs. Instead of killing him and his crew or letting them all die from experimenting with tropical vegetation, the natives pointed out which plants were edible, which lethal. Sweet potatoes, coconuts, avocados, bananas boiled green or eaten ripe and raw, guavas and pineapples have been real treats after a provision-depleting sea voyage. Cashew apples were eaten stewed; cashew nuts were poisonous unless shelled and roasted. *Cassava* (or *yuca* or *manioc*) came in sweet and bitter species, the latter loaded with prussic acid that had to be removed by cooking or pressing. This root could be boiled like a potato or used to make hard, crusty bread as it often is today, by grating, squeezing out the juice through coarse cloth, drying in the sun, cooking on a griddle, then drying again in the sun. Sometimes its poisonous juice was defused and thickened by boiling, making bittersweet *cassareep* to use in spicy pepperpot stew. The natives (misnamed "Indians" by Columbus who believed until his dying day that he had landed in the true Indies not far off the coast of Japan) had no salt, but they had plenty of hot peppers and cassava juice to make their *coui* sauce. They savored the steamy goodness of birds, small animals or fish cooked under hot ashes in a crust of clay, which, when removed, would take with it scales, feathers, skin, quills or fins, leaving only juicy meat and bones. Meat was cooked and cured, too, in strips on a *barbacoa*, a grating of thin green sticks, which some feel must have been the forerunner of the American barbecue. The oil of *annatto*, or *achiote* seeds, was used by the natives to dye their skin a bright orange-red. Later its color and delicate flavor were used like saffron in a sauce, *sofrito*, made by cooking the seeds in hot fat to extract the oil, then adding onions, garlic, cilantro, peppers and other optional ingredients. All kinds of fish, spiny lobsters, huge green turtles ("buffalos of the Caribbean" weighing up to 500 pounds) were the tropical fruits of the sea.

Columbus fascinated all of Europe with tobacco and a few captured natives; but from among the strange new foods, only one resembled the spices of his original dreams: *pimento* berries. These the Europeans named *allspice* because they smelled and tasted so much like a blend of cloves, nutmeg and cinnamon.

A stream of Spanish colonists began to head westward, bringing plants they thought would do well in what became known as the "West Indies": breadfruit, oranges, limes, mangoes, rice, coffee and the crop that turned out most successfully—sugarcane.

The cruel Spanish conquerors turned natives into slaves, non-Spanish-born colonists into second-class citizens. Most of the Arawaks died shortly of disease or committed suicide by drinking uncooked cassava juice. The Caribs successfully massacred numbers of colonists before they fled to the hills or more remote islands.

British, Dutch, French and Danish colonists also laid claim to choice islands, while buccaneers and pirates attacked trading ships around the "Spanish Main." Slavers from 1518 to 1865 are estimated to have brought in 15 million Africans to work in the fields or as house servants. When slavery was abolished, this terrible trade stopped, but more workers were still needed. Willing to assume a social level just barely above the blacks, indentured servants by the thousands were brought in from China and India, thereby adding Oriental delicacies in the form of rice dishes and curries to the West Indian cuisine. Creoles (locally born, but of foreign ancestry) had already added a European touch. Even second-rate Yankee salt fish imported cheaply to sustain the slaves found permanent favor when combined with tropical vegetables or fruits and spicy seasoning. The fact that there are roughly 3,000 edible plants in these tropical isles shows clearly nature's amazing design under the most favorable conditions.

Peasants in the West Indies have suffered through much cruel, hectic and bloody history, but calypso or some other happy magic must have had much to do with their survival. Surely there is no stronger magic than turning dull, nourishing foods into dishes fit for a "could-be" paradise.

WEST INDIES

MOFONGO
Plantain Side Dish

Boil in salted water 15 minutes:
**3 green plantains*, peeled
    and sliced**
Drain, mash and set aside.
Cut into small dice:
**1/4 pound fatty salt pork,
    well rinsed**
Fry until crisp, remove with
slotted spoon and combine with:
mashed plantains
1 garlic clove, finely minced
1 teaspoon cumin powder
Heat salt pork fat remaining in
skillet and spread mixture over
bottom of skillet to cover. Brown
on both sides. Turn over or to
serving dish and cut into wedges.
Good with fish dinner, or for
breakfast with fried eggs.

ASOPAO DE POLLO
Chicken Soup

In heavy soup pot heat:
1/4 cup achiote oil*
Add and sauté 5 minutes:
1 onion, chopped
1 bell pepper, chopped
2 garlic cloves, minced
**1 teaspoon minced fresh
    oregano**
Add and brown on all sides:
1 fryer chicken, cut up
Add:
1 8-ounce can tomato sauce
**3 tablespoons each capers
    and black olives**
1-1/2 cups rice
2 bay leaves
1 teaspoon salt
1/4 teaspoon black pepper
2 quarts boiling water
Cover and simmer 45 minutes.
Then add and simmer 10 minutes:
1 cup fresh peas
**1 sweet red pepper, cut
    in julienne***
Serve in large soup bowls topped
with:
chopped cilantro*
May be made ahead of time.
A meal in itself with bread
and green salad.
Serves 4-6

PAPAS A LA HUNACAÍNA

Dressing for baked or boiled
potatoes, hard-cooked eggs
or green salad.

Heat and stir well to blend:
1/4 cup oil
1/2 teaspoon turmeric
1/8 teaspoon cayenne pepper
Cool and add to:
1/2 pound cottage cheese
**1 3-ounce package cream
    cheese, softened**
1/4 cup evaporated milk
1 tablespoon lime juice
Makes 3 cups

DULCE DE LECHE
Very Sweet Dessert or Topping

Combine and cook over medium
heat until milk curdles:
1 quart milk
**peel from 1 lemon, cut in
    julienne***
1 tablespoon lemon juice
Add:
1 pound brown sugar
Simmer without stirring until
thickened. Serve as dessert or
as topping for ice cream
or custard.

PASTELES
Cabbage-Meat Pies

For batter grate in blender
(in 2 portions):
1/2 pound green plantains*
1 pound each yautias* and
    very green bananas
Pour into large bowl and add:
1/2 cup achiote oil*
1 teaspoon salt
Set aside.
In its own fat brown:
1-1/2 pounds ground beef
    and pork
2 garlic cloves, minced
1 onion, chopped
1 bell pepper, chopped
1 chili pepper (page 17), minced
Add and simmer 15 minutes:
1/2 cup tomato sauce
1 teaspoon each salt and oregano
2 tablespoons capers
1 cup black olives
1/2 teaspoon black pepper

Remove from heat and stir in:
1/4 cup each achiote oil* and
    chopped cilantro leaves*
Mixture will be oily.
Parboil 5 minutes and set aside:
1 large head cabbage
Have available:
12 pimiento-stuffed olives

To assemble pies
Cut aluminum foil into 12-inch
squares and grease centers with
oil from meat mixture. Place
1/4 cup batter on cabbage leaf,
top with 2 tablespoons of the
meat mixture and 1 pimiento-
stuffed olive, and fold cabbage
leaf over filling. Place 'on the
greased foil, fold seams well,
and tuck in ends. Layer the
12 pies in a large pot and cover
with boiling water. Boil gently
1-1/2 hours. May be made ahead
and refrigerated or frozen.
Makes 12

SANCOCHO
Puerto Rican-Style Stew

Brown in:
1/4 cup olive oil
2 pounds pork or beef
    cut into 1-inch cubes
1 onion, chopped
1 garlic clove, minced
Add, cover and simmer 1 hour:
1 quart water
1 teaspoon each salt, cumin
    powder and oregano
1/2 teaspoon black pepper
Peel, grate and form into
1-inch balls:
2 green plantains*
Add to stew pot with:
1 pound each green bananas and
    yautias*, cut into 1-inch cubes
1/2 pound each apio* and
    malanga*, cut up
Cover and cook 30 minutes.
Sancocho appears in many of the
islands.
Serves 4-6

WEST INDIES

HABICUELES GUIDADAS
Puerto Rican-Style Beans

Soak overnight and drain:
2 cups small pink beans
Combine with:
1 onion, chopped
2 garlic cloves, minced
1 quart water
Cover, bring to gentle boil and
simmer 1-1/2 hours. Then add:
**1/4 cup each tomato sauce and
achiote oil***
2 tablespoons chopped cilantro*
1 cup ham, cubed (optional)
1/2 pound calabaza, cubed
(optional)**
Continue cooking, uncovered,
30 minutes to thicken liquid
slightly. Add salt to taste and
spoon over plain steamed rice or
Arroz (page 15). May be made
ahead of time.
Serves 6-8

**Puerto Rican pumpkin, available
in Puerto Rican or Mexican
markets. Substitute Hubbard or
acorn squash; or pumpkin
or yellow squash.

ARROZ CON GANDULES
Rice with Pigeon Peas

Follow directions for **Arroz**
(page 15).
After adding rice to sofrito, add:
**1 1-pound can gandules (pigeon
peas) with its liquid**
2 cups water
1 bay leaf
Cook to absorb liquid, cover and
cook over lowest heat 30 minutes.
Serves 6

ARROZ CON DULCE
Rice Pudding

Combine and simmer 20 minutes:
2 cups water
2 tablespoons whole cloves
2 4-inch pieces stick cinnamon
1 1-inch piece fresh ginger root
Strain into another pot and add:
3 cups coconut milk (page 17)
1/2 cup brown sugar
1/2 teaspoon salt
4 tablespoons butter
**1-1/2 cups rice, washed and
drained**
Stirring frequently, simmer,
uncovered, until rice is tender
and mixture is the consistency
of mush. Then stir in:
1 cup raisins
Pour into a 9x13-inch shallow pan.
Sprinkle with:
**1/2 cup unsalted cracker crumbs
or toasted coconut ***
Chill and cut into squares
to serve.
Serves 6-8

SOPÓN DE GARBANZOS
Garbanzo Bean Soup

Soak overnight and drain:
1/2 pound garbanzo beans
Blanch (page 17) for 5 minutes
and rinse:
2 pounds pigs' feet, cut up
1 pound tripe, cut into 1-inch
  squares
Combine with the drained
garbanzos and:
2 quarts water
Bring to gentle boil, cover
and simmer 1-1/2 hours. Then
add:
1/2 pound pumpkin or Hubbard
  squash, cubed
1/2 pound each diced potatoes
  and chopped cabbage
1 onion, chopped
2 tomatoes, peeled and chopped
1 teaspoon salt
1/2 teaspoon black pepper
1/2 teaspoon chili powder
Continue cooking 45 minutes.
Garnish with chopped fresh
cilantro*.
May be made ahead of time.
Serves 6

GAZPACHO
Avocado-Codfish Salad

Although totally unlike the
Spanish gazpacho, this is the
name used in Puerto Rico.

Soak 8 hours in 4 changes
of water:
1/2 pound salt cod
Discard skin and bones and cut
cod into 1/2-inch dice. Parboil
15 minutes. Drain, rinse in cold
water, drain again and chill.
Parboil until tender but still
firm, any combination of:
green plantains*
yautias*
potatoes
Peel and cut into 1-inch
chunks to make 2 cups.
Marinate while hot in:
1/4 cup oil
2 tablespoons vinegar
1 onion, chopped
Chill. Just before serving add
cod and toss lightly with:
2 bananas, sliced
2 avocados, sliced
Serve on lettuce leaves. This is
a hearty salad—a meal in itself.
Serves 6

PEANUT-RICE SALAD

Combine:
3 cups cooked, cooled rice
1/4 cup each red and green
  minced sweet peppers
1/4 cup chopped green onions
2 tablespoons fresh chopped
  cilantro*
Toss in dressing of:
1/3 cup peanut oil
3 tablespoons lemon juice
1 teaspoon sugar
1/2 teaspoon salt
Mound on lettuce and
surround with:
fresh orange sections
fresh pineapple slices
Sprinkle with:
3/4 cup chopped roasted peanuts

WEST INDIES

BANANA-SWEET POTATO BREAD

Purée in blender:
1/2 cup each cooked
   sweet potatoes and
   very ripe banana
2 eggs
1 tablespoon fresh orange peel
1/4 cup orange juice
4 tablespoons butter
1/2 cup brown sugar
Sift together twice:
2 cups unbleached flour
2 teaspoons baking powder
1 teaspoon baking soda
1/2 teaspoon each salt
   and nutmeg
Combine with potato-banana
mixture and pour into greased
9x5x3-inch loaf pan. Bake in
a 350° oven 40 minutes or until
a toothpick when inserted
comes out clean.

GUMBO

Sauté until crisp:
2 thick slices bacon, diced
Sprinkle with:
2 tablespoons flour
Cook and stir 3 minutes. Then
gradually add:
4 cups water
Cook and stir until smooth,
then add:
4 cups Court Bouillon (page 16)
4 tomatoes, peeled and quartered
2 onions, cut in 1-inch chunks
1 bell pepper, cut in 1-inch chunks
1/2 cup cut-up celery and tops
1/2 pound each zucchini and okra,
   cut up
2 garlic cloves, minced
1 teaspoon each salt and oregano
1/2 teaspoon each black pepper,
   cumin powder and thyme
1-2 chili peppers (page 17), minced
Bring to gentle boil, cover and
simmer 1 hour. Then add:
2 pounds boned, firm fish, cut
   into 1-inch cubes, or
oysters, clams in the shell and/or
raw shrimp in the shell
Cover and simmer 10-15 minutes
until seafood is just done. Do not
overcook. Adjust seasonings and
serve with hot rice.
Serves 8

SOPAS DE BOLAS DE PLÁTANOS
Broth with Plantain Balls

Grate:
1 large green plantain*
Form into 24 small balls and
drop into:
6 cups boiling chicken or
   beef broth
Simmer gently 20 minutes and
garnish with:
chopped cilantro* or
   green onions
Serves 4-6

LATIN AMERICA

WHILE Columbus gave his name to a country, a province, and assorted cities, towns and rivers, a more obscure Italian, Americo Vespucci, bequeathed his monicker—via a German geographer—to the entire western hemisphere. He is said to have exclaimed, "This land is a whole new world!" and it certainly was when it came to foods. The rest of the world widely adopted its avocados, chili peppers, chocolate, lima beans, papayas, peanuts, pineapples, potatoes, pumpkins, sweet potatoes, squash, tomatoes, vanilla and, most important, corn.

Some scientists believe corn, once a wild grass in the Mexican highlands, dates back 60,000 years, about 50,000 years before Asians supposedly found their way across an Alaskan land bridge. Just when these people started cultivating corn is open to speculation, but all the basic types known today were being grown for food when white explorers arrived. For some tribes, corn gods rivaled gods of the sun and moon in importance. *Metates* (grindstones) were common; so were corn festivals, corn dances, prayers for good corn crops, *tamales, tortillas, tacos, enchiladas* and *tostadas*. Together with potatoes, beans and squash, corn provided life-sustaining starch along with valuable fats and proteins. Meat didn't play a large part in the great civilizations of the Mayas, Toltecs, Incas or Aztecs, but food in general did. Some feel the mysterious decline of great jungle and mountain cities may have been related to food shortages.

During their cruel invasion in the 1500's, Spaniards and Portuguese did little to help feed the millions of easily conquered natives. Bananas and sugarcane introduced and raised on huge plantations required hordes of slaves who barely subsisted while the fruits of their labor were exported. Even after the gachupines (Spanish-born colonists), *criollos* (colony-born whites), reds, blacks, *mulattos, mestizos* (red-whites) and *zambos* (red-blacks) threw off the Spanish yoke in 1819, the lot of the peons didn't appreciably improve. To them food has always been a critical problem which they tackled by making something good out of simple foods at hand.

In the high Andes where corn couldn't grow, *chuños*, thinly sliced, frozen, pressed and dried potatoes were an Incan food at least one-half a millenium before present freeze-dried foods. Roasted iguana, *atole* (corn gruel), armadillo meat, dried llama and guinea pig, cooked monkeys, sloths, anteaters and boa constrictors were served as tasty dishes and often still are. For Patagonians (literally, "big feet," a name given them by Magellan) mushrooms are a main-dish staple.

Cookery in Brazil is interwoven with folklore and superstition. Corn possesses virtues that transcend simple nutrition. Beans are good only if cooked in a clay pot. *Cuscuz* here is a molded pudding of toasted *manioc* flour, drowned in coconut milk, sprinkled with grated coconut, finally folded in a banana leaf. The fruit of the *açai* palm is soaked in hot water or "cooked" in the hot sun so the pulp can be worked out. After mixing in a little water it's served in bowls with sugar and *manioc* flour. *Feijoda* is the national dish of black beans and rice. Other countries have their specialties: the *pavsa* (beef broth) of Uruguay, *frijoles* (boiled beans) of Mexico, *locro* (thick corn or potato soup) of Ecuador, *cazuela de ave* (soup with large pieces of chicken, corn, rice, onions, whole potatoes and large green peppers) of Chile, *carbonada criolla* (meat stew with rice and fruit) of Argentina. Seafood dishes abound on every coast and along every river.

For proud peoples to be conquered and named Indians after a land on the other side of the world, then for their lands to be named Latin America after a dead European language and an Italian explorer seems incongruous, to say the least. Ruled by a white minority, these people have had to struggle hard to survive. Their stubborn ability to live on simple foods has helped.

Their unique foods, others from Spain and Portugal and Africa, and the dishes of more recent settlers from all over the world comprise a blended fare of fascinating variety. Though intermarriage has been common, equality has never existed in Latin America. Perhaps sharing cultures and cuisines has helped its common people to live together with relatively little racial strife.

MEXICO

FIDEO
Vermicelli Soup

Sauté until golden in:
**3 tablespoons rendered
    pork fat (page 17)**
**4-6 ounces coil capelini
    (twisted vermicelli),
    broken into small pieces**
Remove with slotted spatula and
set aside. Adding more fat if
needed, sauté until golden:
1 cup chopped onions
1 garlic clove, minced
Add and simmer 20 minutes:
1 quart chicken stock
**1 cup peeled, chopped
    ripe tomatoes**
**2 tablespoons chopped
    red bell pepper**
Add reserved vermicelli, bring
back to boil and cook 3-5
minutes until vermicelli is
al dente (page 17). Sprinkle with:
chopped fresh cilantro*
Serves 4

TORTILLAS MASA
Corn Tortillas

Combine:
2 cups masa harina**
1-1/2 cups water
Knead to blend well. Let rest
30 minutes. Shape into 12 balls
and roll each out into a 6-inch
circle. Cook on hot, lightly-
greased griddle until lightly
browned on both sides.
Makes 12

**prepared corn flour
    available in supermarkets

CHILI CON QUESO
Cheese Sauce

Combine and set aside:
1 egg, beaten
**1/2 pound Monterey Jack cheese,
    shredded or
    imported Asadero or
    Tijuana cheese**
1 teaspoon flour

Heat to boiling:
**2 cups chopped, peeled
    ripe tomatoes**
1 onion, chopped
1/2 teaspoon oregano
1 teaspoon sugar
1 tablespoon vinegar
**1 jalepeno chili (page 17),
    finely minced**
Remove from heat and add
egg-cheese mixture, stirring
constantly to melt cheese. Serve
immediately with:
Corn Tortillas
or beans. Can use leftover
corn tortillas, in which case
deep fry.
Makes 4 cups

FRIJOLES REFRITOS
Refried Beans

Soak overnight and drain:
2 pounds pinto or pink beans
Combine with:
1 onion, chopped
2 teaspoons oregano
3 garlic cloves, minced
1 teaspoon salt
water to cover beans by 1 inch
Bring to gentle boil, cover and
cook over medium heat 1-1/2 hours
or until tender, adding more
water as needed. Last 1/2 hour
of cooking add:
2 tablespoons lard
Mash beans and sauté until
quite dry in:
1/4 cup lard
If desired, cover with grated
Monterey Jack cheese and
broil until cheese is melted.
Serves 6-8

PIMIENTOS FRITOS
Fried Green Peppers

Brown on both sides in:
rendered pork fat (page 17)
bell peppers, seeded and sliced
Serve as a side dish.

LANGUIA ESCAVECHE
Boiled Tongue

In salted water to cover simmer
until tender (about 1-1/2 hours):
1 beef tongue
1 teaspoon oregano
Remove from kettle, cool and
peel. Slice 1/4-inch thick,
dip in:
chili relleno batter (page 144)
and brown on both sides.
Serve with:
Salsa Tomate (page 144)
Serves 6

ENSALADA DE LANGUIA
Tongue Salad

Prepare preceding recipe for:
Boiled Tongue

On platter layer:
sliced tongue
fresh peas, cooked
**   just tender-crisp**
peeled, sliced cucumber
peeled, sliced ripe tomatoes
thinly sliced bell pepper
thinly sliced Bermuda onion
Sprinkle all with:
vinegar and oil to taste
salt and pepper to taste
Garnish with:
chopped cilantro*

HUACHINANGO YUCATÁN
Red Snapper in the Yucatán Way

Sauté until soft in:
3 tablespoons olive oil
1/2 cup chopped onions
Add and cook 4 minutes:
3/4 cup pimiento-stuffed olives
1/2 cup chopped fresh
**   red peppers or bell peppers**
2 tablespoons freshly ground
**   coriander seed**
Add:
1/2 cup each lemon juice and
**   orange juice**
1/2 teaspoon salt
1/4 teaspoon black pepper
In buttered casserole large
enough so as not to crowd, place:
1 4- to 5-pound red snapper,
**   cleaned**
Pour sauce over and bake in
a 375° oven, uncovered,
45 minutes or until tender.
Do not overcook.
Garnish with:
chopped hard-cooked eggs
shredded lettuce
sliced radishes
sliced green onions
Serve with plain rice.
Serves 6

MEXICO

CHAYOTE

This is a squash-like vegetable
available in many markets.

In salted water to cover, boil
until tender:
**2 chayotes, cut in half
lengthwise**
Remove pulp, chop and season
to taste with:
butter
salt and pepper
oregano
Serve with Refried Beans
(page 141) and Salsa Verde.
Serves 4

SALSA VERDE
Green Tomato Sauce

Remove dark outer skin from:
1 pound tomatillos**
Quarter and boil until soft in:
2 cups water
Mash and combine tomatillos
and liquid with:
2 tablespoons chopped cilantro*
1 onion, chopped
1 teaspoon sugar
**1-4 jalepeno chilis (page 17),
minced**
Makes 4 cups

**small green Mexican tomatoes
available in Mexican and some
supermarkets

HUEVOS REVUELTOS
CON CHAYOTE
Chayote Omelet

Beat together and add to
prepared chayote:
6 eggs, beaten
1/4 cup milk
Cook, stirring occasionally,
until eggs are set, in:
2 tablespoons butter
Serves 4

JICAMA

A delicious root vegetable available in many Mexican markets. Best eaten raw. Simply wash, peel, slice thinly, sprinkle with lime juice and refrigerate half an hour. Sprinkle as desired with more lime juice, salt and cayenne pepper.

Or, marinate in lime juice several hours, drain and mix with fresh pineapple, cut up, for a refreshing dessert.

For a salad, marinate several hours in lime juice with sliced green onions, salt and cayenne. Add mayonnaise, seasoned to taste with curry powder, Worcestershire sauce, oil and more lime juice to taste. Adjust with salt and black pepper and serve on lettuce with cooked shrimp or chicken or ham.

MOLÉ POBLANO
**Turkey or Chicken
with Molé Sauce**

In Dutch oven, sauté
5 minutes in:
2 tablespoons lard
2 onions, chopped
2 garlic cloves, minced
Remove with slotted spoon and set aside.

Using more lard as needed, brown on all sides:
1 small turkey, or
1 large roasting chicken or
2 frying chickens, cut up

Transfer to large pot and cover with:
1 quart water
Cover, bring to gentle boil and simmer 45 minutes.
Add back to pot:
reserved onions and garlic
With 1 cup of broth from cooking pot combine all dry ingredients:
**2 tablespoons each chili
powder and flour**
**1 tablespoon dark unsweetened
cocoa**
1 teaspoon cinnamon
**1/4 teaspoon each powdered
cloves and anise seed**
**2 tablespoons each crushed
roasted peanuts and
crushed sesame seeds**
2 teaspoons salt
1/2 teaspoon black pepper
Gradually return to pot and simmer, covered, for 30 minutes. Transfer to heated serving platter. Sprinkle with:
chopped fresh cilantro*
Serves 8

MEXICO

CARNE DE PUERCO
SALSA CHILI/SALSA VERDE
Pork in Hot Tomato Sauce

Cut into 2-inch by 4-inch chunks:
3 pounds pork butt
Rub with mixture of:
2 tablespoons flour
1 tablespoon chili powder
Brown in:
1/4 cup rendered pork fat
(page 17)
Add:
1/2 cup Salsa Chili or
1/2 cup Salsa Verde (page 142)
Cover, lower heat and continue
cooking 30 minutes.
Serve with shredded lettuce in
warmed Corn Tortillas
(page 140).
May be made ahead of time.
Serves 6-8

CHILIS RELLENOS
Chili in Egg Batter

In dry skillet toast, turning
constantly until skin is blistered:
8 long green chili peppers
Remove from heat and immediately
wrap in tea towel (moisture will
soften skin for easy removal). Peel
chilis, make a slit on one side,
remove seeds and stuff with:
1/2 pound Monterey Jack cheese
cut into 8 strips

To make batter, beat until light
and thick:
4 egg yolks
Gradually add:
1/4 cup unbleached flour
Fold in:
4 stiffly beaten egg whites
Heat oil in skillet 1/4-inch deep.
Coat one side of a chili with
2 tablespoons batter, place batter
side down in oil and cover top with
more batter. Fry to brown, turning
once. Do not crowd skillet and add
oil as needed. Drain on paper
toweling and serve with:
Salsa Tomate
Serves 4

SALSA TOMATE
Mild Tomato Sauce

Bring just to boil and simmer
5 minutes:
2 cups chopped, peeled ripe
tomatoes
1 onion, chopped
1 garlic clove, minced
1/2 teaspoon oregano
1 teaspoon sugar
1 tablespoon vinegar
salt and pepper to taste
Makes 3 cups

SALSA CHILI
Hot Tomato Sauce

Prepare preceding recipe for:
Salsa Tomate
Add and cook 5 more minutes:
1-4 hot dried chili peppers,
crushed

HUMAS ENOLLA
Creamed Corn

Sauté until limp in:
2 tablespoons pork lard*
1 onion, minced
1 green pepper, minced
2 small yellow chili peppers
    (page 17), minced or
1/2 teaspoon cayenne pepper
1/2 teaspoon paprika

Grate, reserving corn husks:
7 cups fresh corn,
    about 12 ears
Add to grated corn and
blend thoroughly:
1/3 cup flour
2 tablespoons minced fresh basil
1 teaspoon salt
1/2 teaspoon black pepper
Cook and stir over medium heat
until bubbly, then cook 5 minutes
more. Line a baking dish with
the fresh corn husks. Pour in
hot corn mixture and top with
additional corn husks. Bake in
a 325° oven 30 minutes.
The corn husks will flavor the
dish with a fresh corn taste.
Serve with Ensalada de Tomates
(following recipe).
Serves 8

ENSALADA DE TOMATOES
Tomato Salad

Combine:
3 cups chopped, peeled
    ripe tomatoes
1 cup chopped green onions
1/3 cup oil
3 tablespoons vinegar
1 teaspoon salt
1/2 teaspoon black pepper
Chill and serve.

PASTEL DE CHOCLO
Corn Casserole

Sauté 5 minutes in:
2 tablespoons oil
1 onion, chopped
1/2 cup raisins
1/2 pound chicken, cut into
    1/2-inch dice
1 teaspoon chili powder
Combine:
2 cups grated fresh corn
1 cup milk
2 egg yolks
2 tablespoons each flour and
    melted butter
1 teaspoon sugar
1/2 teaspoon salt
Beat until stiff and fold into
corn mixture:
2 egg whites
In a buttered 2-quart clay
baking dish layer:
chicken mixture
3 hard-cooked eggs, sliced
12 pitted black olives
Pour corn mixture over and bake
in a 350° oven 40 minutes.
Serves 4-6

CHILE

EMPANADAS
Beef Pastries

To make pastry, beat:
1 cup pork lard*
Gradually beat in:
1-1/2 cups hot skim milk
With fork, stir in:
4-1/2 cups unbleached flour
   sifted with
1 teaspoon each salt and
   baking powder
Mix only until blended; do not
knead. Form into ball, cover
with dampened tea towel and
let rest 2 hours.

For filling, brown in:
3 tablespoons pork lard*
1 pound beef round or shank,
   finely minced
Adding more lard if needed,
   sauté until soft:
3-1/2 cups diced onion
2 teaspoons chili powder
1 teaspoon salt
1/2 teaspoon cumin powder
Adjust seasonings to taste and
cool.

Roll pastry 1/8-inch thick and
cut into 36 5-inch rounds.
Place filling on each round,
dividing evenly, and top
each with:
2 softened raisins
1 pitted black olive
1/8th of a hard-cooked egg
Fold over to form half-moon
shape and crimp edges to seal.
Bake in a 375° oven
15-20 minutes until golden.
Or fry in deep fat until golden.

Serve with thinly sliced ripe
tomatoes topped with sliced,
salted onion rings, finely
minced garlic and tiny slivers
of aji peppers*. Pass
powdered sugar.
Serves 12

CHARQUICÁN
Meat and Vegetable Porridge

Heat until garlic starts to
turn golden in:
1/2 cup pork lard*
2 garlic cloves, smashed
Discard garlic and sauté
until soft:
1 cup minced onion
1 bell pepper, minced
1 teaspoon each salt and paprika
1/2 teaspoon each oregano
    and cumin powder
1/4 teaspoon black pepper
Add:
1 pound beef round, minced
8 potatoes, peeled and cut
    lengthwise into 6 pieces

Cover and simmer 30 minutes or
until potatoes are soft.
Then add:
3 carrots, sliced
1 cup green beans, cut into
    2-inch lengths
1/2 pound Hubbard squash, cubed
1/4 cup water
Bring to simmer, cover and
cook 15 minutes. Then add:
1/2 pound fresh peas
kernels cut off 2 ears of corn
4 ripe tomatoes, peeled
    and chopped
Cover and continue cooking
20 minutes. This dish should be
the consistency of a thick
porridge. Top each serving with:
a fried egg
Serve with very sour
pickled cucumbers.
Serves 6

SALSIFY
Oyster Plant

Bring to a boil water, to which
has been added:
salt and lemon slices
Cook in boiling water 15 minutes:
2 large bunches salsify roots *,
    scraped
Drain, reserving water,
and slice.
Melt until bubbly:
2 tablespoons butter
Sprinkle with:
2 tablespoons flour
Cook and stir 3 minutes.
Then gradually add:
1-1/2 cups milk
1/2 cup reserved water
Cook and stir until smooth and
thickened. Add salsify and:
3 tablespoons grated
    Parmesan cheese
Heat to melt cheese and serve
with beef steak and
boiled potatoes.
Serves 6

ARGENTINA

PUCHERO

With variations this one-dish meal could be the national dish of Spain, the Canary Islands, and many other nations. Whole chicken, calf's feet, marrow bones, pumpkin can all be used.

Soak overnight and drain:
1 cup garbanzo beans
Blanch (page 17) 5 minutes and rinse:
1 small smoked pork hock
1 pound beef soup bones
Combine with:
3 quarts water
2 pounds stew meat or
  beef brisket, cut up
Bring to boil, skim off any scum that rises to top and add garbanzo beans and:
2 onions, quartered
1 celery rib and tops, cut up
2 garlic cloves
3 parsley sprigs
6 peppercorns
1 bay leaf
2 teaspoons salt
1/2 teaspoon each oregano
  and cumin powder

Bring to gentle boil, cover and simmer 1-1/2 hours until beef is almost tender. Then add:
1 pound disjointed chicken wings
3 small hot chilis (page 17)
3 potatoes, cut into large chunks
3 turnips, quartered
4 carrots, halved
1 small acorn squash, seeded
  and quartered unpeeled
1 small cabbage cut into 8ths
2 fresh corn cobs, cut into
  2-inch lengths
Bring back to boil and simmer 30 minutes. Last 10 minutes add:
1/2 pound chorizo sausage
Adjust seasonings with salt and pepper. Serve meat, vegetables and broth in separate bowls with lots of minced parsley. Pass Hot Sauce.
Serves 12

HOT SAUCE

Combine:
1/2 cup lemon juice
1-2 aji peppers*, finely minced
2 tablespoons each minced
   onion and parsley
1/4 cup peanut oil
Pass French bread or Brazilian
rice (page 15), Fried Plantains
(page 151) and Mandioca
(see below).
Serves 4-6

MANDIOCA
Buttered Manioc

Sauté to moisten, stirring
constantly in:
1 tablespoon butter
1/2 cup manioc flour*
Grains should stay loose and
dry and absorb a slight buttery
taste. Can add the sieved yolk
of a hard-cooked egg and garnish
with sieved white, minced
parsley, raisins, olives or
diced ham.

FEIJOADA
Black Beans

Soak overnight and drain:
2 cups black beans
Combine soaked beans with:
1 teaspoon salt
1/2 teaspoon black pepper
2 garlic cloves, finely minced
2 ounces salt pork, diced
1 meaty pig's foot, cut up
   (approximately 1 pound)
2-1/2 cups canned tomatoes
1 onion, chopped
4 cups water
Bring to gentle boil, cover and
simmer 1-1/2 hours, adding more
water if needed. Then add:
1 12-ounce linguica or chorizo
   sausage, sliced
Cook uncovered until liquid has
thickened and sausage is cooked.
Serve with cold sliced oranges,
cooked fresh kale and Brazilian
rice (page 15). Pass Mandioca
(preceding recipe). May be made
ahead of time.
Serves 6-8

FLAN
Custard Dessert

In heavy skillet, over medium
heat, carmelize (cook until it
turns into a brown syrup):
3/4 cup sugar
Coat a 1-1/2-quart baking dish
with the caramel and set aside.

Scald and cool to lukewarm:
3 cups milk
1 tablespoon butter
Beat together:
5 eggs
3 tablespoons sugar
1/2 teaspoon vanilla extract,
rum or coconut flavoring
1/4 teaspoon almond extract
Blend into milk, pour over
caramel, place baking dish in
a pan filled with hot water
to reach halfway up sides, and
bake in a 375° oven
45 minutes or until set. Cool,
refrigerate and turn out
onto serving dish.
Serves 8

BRAZIL

REFOGADO
Tomato Sauce with Cornmeal

Sauté until soft in:
3 tablespoons oil
2 onions, chopped
2 garlic cloves, finely minced
1/2 cup minced bell pepper
Add and cook 5 minutes:
1 cup chopped fresh
    ripe tomatoes
1 teaspoon salt
1/2 teaspoon each sugar and
    black pepper
Add and cook 5 minutes:
1/4 teaspoon cumin powder
1/2 teaspoon oregano
1-2 aji peppers *, finely minced

Set aside and keep warm.
Remove half the mixture to
another saucepan; to remaining
mixture add:
1-1/4 cups water
Bring to boil and gradually
stir in:
1/2 cup yellow cornmeal
Cook and stir over medium heat
until very thick, about
5 minutes. Cover, lower heat and
simmer 15-20 minutes. Turn out
onto heated platter, surround
with fried ham and vegetables
such as sweet potatoes, summer
squash, corn on the cob and
carrots. Pour reserved
sauce over.
Serves 6

GAUCHO CHURRASSCO
Brazilian Barbecue

Combine:
1/2 cup lemon juice
1/2 teaspoon salt
1/4 teaspoon black pepper
Add and marinate overnight:
2 pounds beef and/or lamb
    hearts, cut in 1-1/2-inch
    chunks
Drain meat and skewer
alternately with:
linguica or chorizo sausages,
    cut into 1-inch lengths
Grill over charcoal or wood fire
5 minutes on each side until
cooked but still juicy.
Serve with Hot Sauce (page 149).

ENSALADA DE VERANO
Fresh Salad with
Avocado Dressing

Combine:
1 cup mashed ripe avocados
1/4 cup tomato purée
1/2 teaspoon aji peppers *,
　finely minced
1/2 teaspoon Worcestershire
　sauce
1/2 teaspoon sugar
1/2 cup olive oil
1/4 cup vinegar
2 hard-cooked eggs, chopped
Adjust seasonings to taste and
serve on lettuce with raw
vegetables such as:
carrots
zucchini
peas
cauliflower
cucumbers
Makes 2 cups dressing

SOPA DE QUESO
Cheese Soup

Dissolve in:
2 cups milk
2 tablespoons cornstarch
Add and bring to boil:
4 cups chicken stock
Add:
1 cup cubed Monterey Jack
　cheese
Cook and stir until cheese is
just melted. Sprinkle with:
3 hard-cooked eggs,
　finely minced
1/4 cup minced parsley
2 tablespoons butter bits
black pepper
Serves 6

FRIED PLANTAINS

As accompaniment to foods
(especially hot ones) serve
bananas or ripe plantains*,
halved lengthwise and browned
on both sides in butter, oil or
pork lard*. If serving for dessert
pass sour cream.

**FRIJOLES CON TOCINO
Y MAZORCA**
Beans and Corn

Soak 2 hours and drain:
2 cups navy beans
Combine soaked beans with:
1/4 pound slab bacon, cubed
2 teaspoons fresh basil
1 bay leaf
1/2 teaspoon black pepper
water to cover
Bring to boil, cover and cook
1-1/2 hours or until tender,
adding water as needed.
Add and continue cooking
15 minutes:
1 cup fresh corn kernels
1 teaspoon salt
Serves 6-8

COLUMBIA

TORTILLA DE JAMON Y LANGOSTINOS
Ham and Shrimp Omelet

Combine:
6 eggs, beaten
1 cup milk
2 tablespoons melted butter
1 teaspoon cornstarch
1/2 teaspoon salt
1 cup shredded mild cheese
1 cup cooked diced prawns
1 cup cooked diced ham
1/2 cup chopped tomatoes
1 cup cooked rice
Bake in a 350° oven
40 minutes until eggs are set
and top is brown.
Serves 6

POLLO CON ARROZ A LA CRIOLLA
Chicken and Pork with Rice

Sauté in:
2 tablespoons pork lard *
1 cup chopped onion
Add and brown:
1 pound cubed lean pork butt
1 chicken, cut up
Add:
4 tomatoes, chopped
1 cup raw rice
1-1/2 cups water
1/2 teaspoon each salt and saffron
1/4 teaspoon black pepper
Bring to boil, cover and cook
over medium-low heat 30 minutes,
adding water if needed.
Then add:
2 cups fresh string beans, sliced very thinly on diagonal
1 cup fried chopped chorizo sausage
Bring back to boil and cook
10 minutes or until beans are
tender. Adjust seasonings with
salt and pepper. May be made
ahead of time.
Serves 6

POSTRE DE MANZANAS CON COCO
Baked Apples with Coconut

Place in skillet in 1 layer:
10 whole apples, peeled and cored
Sprinkle with:
2 tablespoons lemon juice
1/2 cup sugar
2 cups boiling water
Cover and steam for 10 minutes
or until tender.
Cool and fill with mixture of:
1 cup shredded sweet coconut *
1/4 cup each port and honey
Beat until stiff:
2 egg whites
Add:
1/4 cup sugar
Transfer apples to buttered
baking dish and top with egg
and sugar meringue. Bake in
a 425° oven 15 minutes to
heat apples and brown meringue.
Serve immediately.
Serves 10

NORTH AMERICA

I N CANADA and the United States home-prepared food is often categorized by ancestral ethnic groups. Many favorite dishes are handed-down reproductions of, or improvements on, great grandma's recipe from the old country. Of course, there has been much trading and mixing of traditional cuisines through the years while the melting pot simmered.

According to one theory it was French voyageurs living like Indians who named that great American institution, the barbecue, as they roasted whole animals spitted from barbe (whiskers) to queue (tail). Except for haphazardly cultivated corn, Indians depended mostly on game, fish and other wild provender. Though feast or famine could result, generally they ate quite well. By grinding, soaking, stewing, baking and seasoning with herbs, most tribes developed cooking into an art, not merely a means of survival.

On the Atlantic coast clams and lobsters were baked-steamed over hot rocks under a seaweed blanket. Puritans were quick to adopt the clambake and used a similar method for avoiding cooking on the Sabbath. A pot of beans placed in a bean-hole on a bed of embers then covered with earth on a Saturday night reached steaming perfection just in time for Sunday dinner.

In the South, soups, opossum stew, shrimp, cornbread (pone, hoecake, spoon bread) and hominy grits (boiled center of milled corn, ground into grits) were considered tasty fare. Around northern lakes, still famous for their fish, could be found two great delicacies: turtles and turtle eggs, also wild rice, or water oats. Plains Indians, especially after horses arrived from Spain, could always enjoy a bison roast or stew—reputedly better than beef—or wing a game bird more flavorful than chicken.

In the arid Southwest, Hopis, Pueblos and Papagos (bean people) enjoyed many of the same foods, by irrigating, as did their Mexican neighbors, especially chili peppers, squash, beans and corn. The Pueblo calendar of today is still marked with Corn and Turtle Dances, Elk, Buffalo, Deer Dances, Green Corn Dances, Spring Corn Dances, Summer Corn Dances, and just plain Corn Dances.

Seed gatherers living in the dry hills and valleys of California and Nevada of necessity became great basket weavers. The Hoopa Acorn Festival today is celebrated every September, for acorns, pounded to a coarse flour and baked into bread, were long these Indians' principal food. Piñon nuts were sweet; wild plant seeds were easy to eat; occasional rabbits, deer and antelopes were special treats. Some tribes resorted to boiled or roasted grasshoppers for food.

In the Pacific Northwest, stretching from the California border to Alaska, Indians seemed to fare the best. Seafood, wild greens, fruit and game were so plentiful a whole year's supply of food could be gathered in three months. Red caviar added a luxurious touch, juniper berries a unique flavor. Chieftans flaunted their wealth and strength by inviting each other to great feasts and festivals called *potlatches* (from *potshatl*, gift). Not only would quantities of food be consumed, but gifts would be distributed and the host would prove his wealth by publicly destroying valued possessions.

Meat assumed its greatest importance farther north in Canada and Alaska, for large animals were more efficient fishers, hunters of small game and gatherers of sparse vegetation than man. Also, they offered bigger targets and meals. Eskimos and Aleuts found necessary proteins and fats in turtles, snakes, large mammals of the sea, bears and the large game peculiar to North America: caribou, elk and moose.

That man ranks most destructive among predators is well demonstrated by the near extinction of a tremendous source of food, the bison. Less familiar is the complete demise of the succulent passenger pigeon, so plentiful three generations ago that flocks would darken the sky, so easily butchered that a dozen would bring only fifteen to twenty-five cents on the wholesale market. Their extinction has a different twist. The pigeons were great chestnut eaters, until 1904 when a blight from Japanese chestnut trees spread many times faster than the Dutch elm blight and destroyed America's chestnuts, sweeter than European. Caught between slaughter and lack of food the passenger pigeon, one of the world's best peasant foods, quickly disappeared.

Luckily other imports such as sheep, hogs, cattle, chickens, wheat and rice fared better—in fact so well that few modern American peasants need be without **meat** or nourishing food of some kind, if they stick to basics instead of expensive processed foods.

Nowhere other than in the United States and Canada has there been made available to more people such a wide variety of edibles through ethnic heritage, fertile land, and miracles of modern technology—preservation, storage, transportation and manufacturing. Even the poor can pick and choose. Together with gourmets they can explore various cultures of the world, past and present, through re-creating special dishes of most all the world's peoples.

CANADA

SPLIT PEA SOUP

Soak 2 hours and drain:
2 cups yellow split peas
Sauté in:
2 tablespoons bacon drippings
1 garlic clove, minced
1 onion, chopped
1/2 cup chopped celery and tops
Add drained split peas and:
2 quarts water
1 teaspoon salt
1/4 teaspoon black pepper
1 bay leaf
Bring to gentle boil, cover
and simmer 1 hour. Then add:
2 cups potatoes, cut into
**   1/2-inch dice**
Simmer 30 minutes, discard
bay leaf and sprinkle with:
3 pieces bacon, cooked crisp
**   and crumbled**
Serve with Potato Bread
(page 10).
Serves 6

CORN AND CABBAGE SOUP

Bring to boil:
6 cups rich beef broth
Add:
1/2 small cabbage, coarsely
**   shredded**
Bring back to boil, cook
10 minutes and add:
2 cups fresh corn kernels
Reheat and sprinkle with
minced parsley.
Serves 6

PEAS IN THE POD

A friend from Quebec says young
tender peas in the pod can be
messy but marvelous! Simply
cook in a little sugared water
until tender-crisp, drain, add
salt and lots of butter and
steam to blend. Eat with
fingers, putting entire pod in
the mouth and stripping through
the teeth to extract all the
taste of the pod and the peas,
too!

TOURTIÈRE
Pork Pie

Line a 9-inch pie plate with
half of:
double recipe of Biscuit Pastry
**   Dough (page 13)**
Sauté:
2 slices bacon, diced
1 onion, minced
1 garlic clove, minced
When onions start to turn
golden add:
1 pound ground pork
1 teaspoon salt
1/2 teaspoon pepper
1/4 teaspoon powdered cloves
2 tablespoons chopped parsley
Brown, stirring often. Then add
and cook, covered, 15 minutes:
1/4 cup water
Sprinkle with:
1 tablespoon flour
Stir well and pour into pastry
shell. Cover with top crust,
make several slits in top and
bake in a 425° oven
30 minutes or until crust is
golden brown. Serve hot or cold.
Serves 4-6

ROAST WILD GOOSE

Prick skin well to release
fat of:
1 wild goose
Marinate at least 4 hours
in a mixture of:
1 cup dry white wine
**1/4 cup each lemon and
    orange juice**
2 tablespoons apricot jam
1/8 teaspoon nutmeg
Remove goose from marinade
and sprinkle generously inside
and out with:
salt and pepper
Stuff with:
1 large parsley sprig
2 celery tops
1 onion studded with 2 cloves
Place on rack in roasting pan;
roast in a 425° oven,
basting occasionally with pan
juices, 30 minutes. Reduce heat
to 375° and continue roasting
and basting every 15 minutes
for 45 minutes or until tender.
Remove to heated platter and
keep warm. Add marinade to
pan and cook rapidly to reduce
by half. Pour over goose and
serve with:
Brown Rice Stuffing
Poached Pears and Prunes
Serves 4-6

BROWN RICE STUFFING

Sauté in:
1 tablespoon bacon drippings
1 onion, chopped
Add and brown:
1/2 pound bulk pork sausage
Add:
1 tart apple, pared and chopped
**2 tablespoons each chopped
    celery tops and parsley**
**1/4 teaspoon each sage and
    marjoram**
1 cup chicken broth
Cover and cook over medium heat
10 minutes. Then add and
mix well:
3 cups hot cooked brown rice
Makes 6 cups

POACHED PEARS
AND PRUNES

Bring to boil, then simmer
20 minutes:
1-1/2 cups water
**1/2 cup each port and
    red wine**
3/4 cup brown sugar
4 whole cloves
3 3-inch cinnamon sticks
6 pitted prunes
**4-6 large pears, peeled, cored
    and quartered**
Remove pears and prunes with
slotted spoon. Pour syrup over
fruit and serve hot or cold.

SAGE HEN (GROUSE)

Cut into serving pieces:
1 large or 2 medium sage hens
Sprinkle pieces with a
mixture of:
2 tablespoons flour
**1/2 teaspoon each salt
    and thyme**
1/4 teaspoon black pepper
Brown slowly on both sides in:
2 tablespoons corn oil
Add:
1/2 cup grated carrot
1 onion, chopped
1/2 cup chicken stock
Cover and simmer 20-30 minutes
or until tender.
Serves 4-6

157

CANADA

BLUEBERRY COFFEE CAKE

Cream thoroughly:
4 tablespoons butter
3/4 cup sugar
1 egg
Add:
1/2 cup milk
Sift together and add:
2 cups unbleached flour
2 teaspoons baking powder
1/2 teaspoon salt
Carefully fold in:
2 cups fresh blueberries
Batter will be thick. Pour into
a greased 9-inch square pan.
Crumble together:
1/3 cup each brown sugar and
    unbleached flour
4 tablespoons butter
1/2 teaspoon cinnamon
1/4 teaspoon nutmeg
Add:
1/2 cup chopped nuts
Sprinkle over batter and bake in
a 375° oven 1 hour. Serve
warm. Good for breakfast or
afternoon tea or coffee.

PEPPER POT SOUP

Cut into strips, blanch (page 17)
   5 minutes, and set aside:
2 pounds honeycomb tripe
Sauté 5 minutes in:
2 tablespoons butter
1 tart apple, pared and diced
3/4 cup chopped celery and tops
2 onions, diced
Add reserved tripe and:
2 quarts water
1 veal or beef knuckle
1 bell pepper, diced
1/2 teaspoon black peppercorns
1/4 cup minced parsley
1 teaspoon each salt and sugar
1/4 teaspoon each marjoram
   and sage
1/8 teaspoon each thyme and
   cayenne pepper
Bring to boil, cover and simmer
45 minutes. Then add and cook
20 minutes:
2 cups diced potatoes
Blend together and gradually
add to soup:
1/3 cup flour
1 5-1/3-ounce can
   evaporated milk
Cook and stir until soup is
slightly thickened, remove
knuckle and just before serving
swirl in:
1 tablespoon butter
Serves 8-10

TRADITIONAL BAKED BEANS

Soak overnight and drain:
2 cups small white beans
In bean pot layer soaked beans
and:
1/2 pound salt pork, blanched
   (page 17) 5 minutes and sliced
2 onions, diced
Sprinkle each layer with
mixture of:
1/4 cup brown sugar
2 teaspoons dry mustard
End layering with salt pork and
pour over it a mixture of:
3 cups boiling water
1/2 cup dark molasses
2 teaspoons salt
1/2 teaspoon black pepper
Cover tightly and bake in a
275° oven 8 hours, checking
occasionally to add more boiling
water as needed. Last half hour
of cooking remove cover. Serve
with Boston Brown Bread.
Serves 6-8

BOSTON BROWN BREAD

Sift together:
2 cups whole wheat flour
2 teaspoons each baking powder,
   baking soda and salt
Blend in:
1 cup yellow cornmeal
3/4 cup dark molasses
2 cups buttermilk
Fold into batter:
1 cup raisins, tossed in
1 tablespoon flour
Pour batter into 2 1-pound
greased coffee tins, cover
tightly with heavy foil and
place on rack or plate in large
kettle. Fill kettle with
boiling water 3/4 up sides of
cans, cover and steam, keeping
water gently boiling,
2-1/2 hours. Add more boiling
water if level goes down. Lift
cans from water, remove foil
and let stand 5 minutes. Turn
out on rack and serve warm or
cooled. Serve with butter or
cream cheese.

NEW ENGLAND BOILED DINNER

Cover with cold water:
**1 5-pound corned beef
  brisket, rinsed**
Bring to boil and blanch
(page 17) 5 minutes. Discard
water, rinse, cover with cold
water and add:
1 onion studded with 2 cloves
1 carrot
1 celery rib with leaves
12 peppercorns
2 bay leaves
6 parsley sprigs
1 thyme sprig or
  1/2 teaspoon thyme
1/4 pound salt pork, rinsed
Bring just to boil, cover and
simmer 2-1/2 hours or until
meat is tender. Uncover, cool
and refrigerate overnight.
Remove fat, take out meat and
reheat stock; strain and return
meat. Bring just to boil and
add:

6 whole carrots
1/2 teaspoon dry mustard
Cook 10 minutes and add:
12 small onions
6 medium potatoes
3 parsnips, halved (optional)
Cook 10 minutes and add:
1/2 medium cabbage, quartered
Cook until cabbage is
tender-crisp. Serve with
a sprinkling of minced parsley
and chives and a side dish of
beets cooked and dressed with
vinegar.
Serves 6-8

RED FLANNEL HASH

Chop leftovers from preceding
recipe for New England Boiled
Dinner and fry in bacon
drippings or oil. Top with
a poached egg.

PORK CAKE

Combine:
**1/2 pound salt pork, rinsed
  and finely minced**
1/2 cup dark molasses
3/4 cup sugar
1 cup hot strong coffee
1 teaspoon baking soda

Sift together:
2 cups unbleached flour
1 teaspoon cinnamon
1/2 teaspoon ginger
**1/4 teaspoon each powdered
  cloves and allspice**
Add to salt pork mixture,
then fold in:
1 cup raisins
Pour into well-greased 8-inch
square pan and bake in a 350°
oven 50 minutes or until
a toothpick when inserted
comes out clean. Cool on cake
rack, turn out and serve warm
or cold. For festive occasions
add 1/2 cup citron or candied
orange peel to batter. This cake
keeps well if wrapped and
refrigerated, especially if
1/3 cup port or dry sherry is
poured over and allowed to
seep in.

PERSIMMON PUDDING

Sift together:
1-1/2 cups flour
2 teaspoons each baking powder
   and baking soda
1 teaspoon salt
Purée in blender:
1 cup persimmon pulp (from
   2 or 3 very ripe persimmons)
1 cup chopped walnuts
2 tablespoons butter
1/4 cup milk
1 teaspoon vanilla
Mix into flour and blend well
to make thick batter. Pour into
greased 1-1/2-quart mold.
Cover mold tightly and steam
3 hours, keeping water gently
boiling. Add more boiling water
if level goes down. Remove mold
and turn out on plate.
Serve warm with Custard Sauce.
Serves 8-10

CUSTARD SAUCE

Combine:
1/4 cup flour
1/3 cup sugar
1-1/2 cups milk
Stir and cook until almost to
boil and slightly thickened.
Remove from heat and
gradually beat into half the
milk mixture:
3 eggs, beaten
Return to rest of milk, heat
and stir constantly until
mixture starts to boil. Remove
from heat and stir in:
1 tablespoon rum or brandy

APPLESAUCE MOLASSES CAKE

Dissolve in:
1 tablespoon warm water
1 teaspoon baking soda
Combine with:
1 cup applesauce
1/2 cup sugar
1/2 cup dark molasses
1/2 cup softened shortening

Sift together:
2 cups unbleached flour
1/2 teaspoon each salt and
   cinnamon
1/4 teaspoon each powdered
   cloves and nutmeg
Add to applesauce mixture with:
1 cup raisins or currants
1/2 cup chopped walnuts
   (optional)
Turn into well-greased 8-inch
square pan and bake in a 350°
oven 50-60 minutes or until
a toothpick inserted comes
out clean. Serve warm, plain,
with hard sauce, or whipped
cream, or a sprinkling of
powdered sugar or vanilla
ice cream.

UNITED STATES/PENNSYLVANIA DUTCH

SCHNITZ UN KNEPP
Apples and Pork Chops

In water to cover soak 4 hours
or more:
1-1/2 cups dried apples
Rub into:
6 thick pork chops
1/2 teaspoon black pepper
In their own fat brown chops on
both sides. Then add:
1-1/2 cups water
drained apples
Bring to gentle boil, cover and
simmer 30 minutes. Make:
dumplings, recipe following
and drop by tablespoonfuls
into pot. Cover tightly and
cook 10 minutes.
Serves 6

SHAKER SALT COD DINNER

Blanch (page 17) 5 minutes
and rinse:
1 pound salt cod
Place in kettle with:
6 medium onions
6 potatoes, peeled
Bring to boil, cover and
simmer 1/2 hour. In another pot
cook until tender in:
salted water to cover
6 beets

To make white sauce, melt until
bubbly:
3 tablespoons butter
Sprinkle with:
3 tablespoons flour
Cook and stir 3 minutes,
gradually adding:
2 cups milk
1/2 teaspoon salt
1/4 teaspoon black pepper
1/8 teaspoon nutmeg
When potatoes are soft remove
and mash with:
2 tablespoons butter
1/2 cup milk
Remove and keep warm.
Peel and slice beets.
Remove cod and place on center
of heated platter. Arrange the
onions, mashed potatoes and
beets around the cod and pour
the white sauce over all.
Sprinkle with lots of minced
parsley and serve with Red
Beet Eggs.
Serves 6

RED BEET EGGS

Combine and cook 10 minutes:
**1 cup beet juice (water in which
    3-4 beets have been cooked
    tender)**
1 cup vinegar
2 tablespoons sugar
3/4 teaspoon salt
**1/4 teaspoon each powdered
    cloves, allspice and nutmeg**
Pour over to cover completely:
8 hard-cooked eggs
Let stand at least 4 hours; the
longer they marinate, the
spicier they become. Can be
refrigerated up to 1 week.
Pickling juice is also good
served over cooked sliced beets.

RED FISH HASH

To each cup of chopped leftovers
from Shaker Salt Cod Dinner add:
2 tablespoons minced onion
1 egg, beaten
Brown slowly in bacon drippings,
turning once. Serve for
breakfast (good color for
Christmas) with a poached egg
per person, or as a luncheon
dish with beet greens cooked
with garlic.

PONHAUS

Combine:
1 pound pigs' feet, cut up
2 pounds pork scraps (jowl,
    butt and/or shoulder) blanched
    (page 17) 5 minutes, drained
    and cut up
6 cups water
1 teaspoon salt
8 peppercorns
4 whole cloves
1 bay leaf
Bring to boil, cover and simmer
2 hours or until tender. Strain,
chop meat and reserve. Skim as
much fat as possible off surface
of broth.
Combine:
1 cup each cornmeal and
    rolled oats
1/4 teaspoon cayenne pepper
1/2 teaspoon each nutmeg, sage
    and marjoram
Reheat broth and slowly add
grain mixture. Cook and stir
over low heat 15 minutes until
thickened. Add reserved meat and
pour into 2 greased loaf pans.
Cool, cover and refrigerate.

To serve, turn loaf onto board,
slice 1/2-inch thick, roll
slices in cornmeal and brown
both sides in bacon or sausage
drippings. Serve with maple
syrup, molasses or brown sugar,
applesauce or fried apple
slices, or poached eggs. This is
a rich, hearty breakfast.
It keeps well and can be frozen.
Serves 8-10

BOOVA SHENKEL
Beef Stew with Dumplings

Bring to boil:
2 pounds lean beef stew meat,
    cut into 1-inch cubes
3 cups water
1 teaspoon salt
1/2 teaspoon black pepper
Cover and simmer 1-1/2 hours or
until meat is tender.
Prepare:
1 recipe dumpling dough
Divide in half and shape each
half into a long oval to fit
the stew pot. Place dumplings
on top of meat, cover pot tightly
and cook over medium heat
15 minutes. Do not remove lid
while cooking dumplings.
Serve with Parsley Potatoes.
Serves 6

PARSLEY POTATOES

Boil until tender in:
salted water to cover
6 medium potatoes
Peel, slice and while still hot,
add:
2 tablespoons softened butter
1 onion, minced
2 tablespoons minced parsley
2 eggs, beaten
1/2 teaspoon salt
1/4 teaspoon black pepper

DUMPLINGS

Sift together:
1 cup sifted unbleached flour
2 teaspoons baking powder
1/2 teaspoon salt
Add:
1/2 cup milk
2 teaspoons oil or melted fat
Mix with a fork until
just blended.

HOPPING JOHN
Black-Eyed Peas

In the most elegant or humble
of Southern homes, this is
a traditional New Year's Day
dish assuring good luck for
the forthcoming year.

Soak overnight and drain:
1 cup cow (black-eyed) peas
Combine soaked peas with:
4 cups water
1 onion, chopped
1/4 pound meaty salt pork,
    blanched (page 17) 5 minutes
    and sliced
Bring to boil, cover and simmer
2 hours, adding boiling water
if needed to leave at least
1/2 cup liquid in pot when
beans are done.
Stir in:
2 cups hot steamed rice
Serve as meat accompaniment.
Good with ham hocks and
collard greens cooked together.
Serves 6

CORN OYSTERS (FRITTERS)

Combine:
4 eggs, beaten
2 cups fresh corn kernels
6 tablespoons flour
1 teaspoon salt
1/4 teaspoon black pepper
1/4 cup crumbled, crisp
    cooked bacon (optional)
2 tablespoons finely minced
    green onion and/or
    bell pepper
In heavy skillet heat:
2 tablespoons bacon drippings
Drop batter by tablespoons
into skillet and brown over
medium heat. Turn to brown
other side, remove and drain on
paper toweling. Repeat, using
more fat as needed. Serve as
an accompaniment to chicken or
beef pot roast.
Makes 16-20, serves 4

SWEETBREADS
AND OYSTER PIE

Have ready:
1 pound parboiled sweetbreads,
    trimmed and sliced
1 pint oysters, drained and
    halved if large

2 hard-cooked eggs, sliced
1 tablespoon each chopped
    green onions and parsley

In a saucepan melt:
2 tablespoons butter or
    chicken fat
Blend in:
2 tablespoons flour
Gradually stir in:
1 cup milk
Season with:
1/2 teaspoon salt
1/4 teaspoon each paprika
    and nutmeg
1/8 teaspoon cayenne pepper
Stir and cook sauce for
10 minutes, remove from heat
and add:
1 tablespoon dry sherry
In buttered deep 1-1/2-quart
baking dish, layer half the
prepared ingredients in order
given. Sprinkle first layer
with:
1 tablespoon flour
Repeat layer and pour cream
sauce over all. Top with:
Biscuit Pastry Dough (page 13)
Prick in several places to allow
steam to escape. Bake in a
400° oven 45 minutes until
golden.
Serves 6

CUSTARD CORN CAKE

Combine:
3 eggs, beaten until frothy
4 cups milk
1 teaspoon salt

Sift together:
1 cup yellow cornmeal
2 teaspoons baking soda
1 tablespoon sugar

Measure half the egg-milk mixture and add to cornmeal with:
2 tablespoons corn oil or melted chicken fat
Turn into a greased 2-quart baking dish and slowly pour remaining egg-milk mixture on top. Bake in a 375° oven, stirring 3 times at 5-minute intervals. Continue baking 45 minutes or until top is golden brown and crust has formed. The custard may rise to the top or stay in center; delicious either way.
Serves 6-8

TEXAS CHILI

Brown in:
1/4 cup minced beef suet
2 pounds beef stew meat cut into 1/2-inch dice
1 onion, minced
2 garlic cloves, minced
Add:
1 bay leaf
1 6-ounce can tomato paste
1-1/2 cups water
1 tablespoon each sugar, paprika and instant coffee
1 teaspoon each oregano and salt
1/2 teaspoon each black pepper and cumin powder
1 to 4 crushed dried hot red peppers
Bring to boil, cover and simmer 1-1/2 hours or until beef is tender.

Sprinkle with:
1-1/2 tablespoons masa harina**
Cook and stir 5 minutes to thicken slightly.
Sprinkle with:
finely minced raw onions or grated Monterey Jack cheese
Serve with freshly cooked rice, warmed corn tortillas, or Texas Beans.
Serves 6-8
**prepared corn flour available in supermarkets

TEXAS BEANS

Soak overnight and drain:
2 cups pinto or kidney beans
Sauté until golden in:
6 tablespoons lard
2 onions, minced
2 garlic cloves, minced
6 cups water
1 teaspoon each salt and oregano
1/4 teaspoon cayenne pepper
Bring to boil, cover and simmer 2 hours until tender.
Serves 6

PINTO BEAN SOUP

Soak 2 hours and drain:
1 pound pinto beans
Combine soaked beans with:
3 quarts water
2 pounds meaty beef soup bones
1 large onion cut into 8ths
2 garlic cloves, minced
2 teaspoons salt
bouquet garni of:
   2 bay leaves
   6 peppercorns
   1/2 teaspoon coriander seeds
   1 small dried chili pepper
   (page 17), crushed
Bring to boil, cover and simmer
2 hours or until meat and beans
are tender. Discard bouquet
garni, remove shanks, cut up
the meat and return it to
the soup. Reheat and serve with
Buckskin Flat Bread.
Serves 8

INDIAN ORANGES

Loosen sections of:
6 oranges, cut in half
Spoon over each half:
1 teaspoon honey
Put halves together and
refrigerate 24 hours or more.
Serve 2 halves per person,
garnishing with sprigs of mint.
Serves 6

INDIAN SUNFLOWER SEED COOKIES

Cream until well blended:
1/4 pound butter or
1/2 cup corn oil
3/4 cup brown sugar
1 egg
1/2 teaspoon vanilla
Sift together and add:
3/4 cup unbleached flour
1/2 teaspoon each baking soda
   and salt
Add:
1-1/2 cups rolled oats
3/4 cup sunflower seeds, shelled
Drop by teaspoonfuls onto
greased cookie sheets. Bake
in a 350° oven 10 minutes.
Makes 48

INDIAN BUCKSKIN FLAT BREAD

Combine:
2 cups whole wheat flour
1 teaspoon each baking powder
   and salt
1 cup water
Press into lightly greased pie
tin and bake in a 400° oven
25-30 minutes. Remove and break
into pieces. Serve with butter,
as accompaniment for soup or
stew.
Serves 4

INDIAN CARROT BREAD

Combine and bring to boil:
2 cups grated carrots
3/4 cup water
Cook over medium heat until
tender, remove from heat
and add:
2 tablespoons each honey,
    brown sugar and butter
1 cup cornmeal
3/4 cup milk
Sift together:
1-1/2 cups whole wheat flour
1/2 teaspoon baking soda
1 teaspoon each baking
    powder and salt
Combine with carrot mixture,
turn into a buttered 8-inch
square pan and bake in a 350°
oven 50 minutes or until
a toothpick when inserted comes
out clean. Serve hot with
butter. So moist it must be
eaten with a fork.

GREEN TOMATO RELISH

Combine:
4 cups sliced green tomatoes
2 onions, sliced
3-4 cups shredded cabbage
1 cup celery, thinly sliced
2-1/2 tablespoons salt
water to cover
Let stand 1 hour, drain, rinse
and drain again. Then add:
1 large red pepper, sliced
1 large green pepper, sliced
2 cups cider vinegar
3/4 cup brown sugar
1 tablespoon white mustard seeds
12 whole cloves
10 allspice berries
20 peppercorns
1 4-inch stick cinnamon
1 sprig fresh dill
Bring to boil, cover and simmer
15 minutes, stirring
occasionally. Ladle into
sterilized jars, seal and cool.
Good with any meat or poultry.
Makes 4 cups

APPLE AND YAM BAKE

Boil until tender in
salted water to cover:
4 medium yams
Cool, peel and slice. Then peel
and slice:
enough tart apples to fill
    3 cups
Arrange half the apples in
a greased baking dish, top with
half the yam slices and
sprinkle with:
2 tablespoons brown sugar
1/4 teaspoon salt
2 tablespoons butter bits
Repeat layers, pour over:
1/2 cup cider
Cover tightly and bake in
a 400° oven 15 minutes.
Remove cover, baste with juices
and bake and baste 10 more
minutes. Serve with baked ham.
Serves 4-6

FIG APPETIZER

Fry until crisp:
12 slices bacon
Place two pieces on each of
6 plates and arrange on each:
3 fresh figs
Pass the peppermill.
Serves 6

FRESH ROE CAKES

Combine:
2 eggs, beaten
1 tablespoon each water
   and flour
2 tablespoons minced green onion
1/2 cup chopped fresh spinach
1/2 teaspoon salt
1 cup raw fish roe (from
   cod, bass, etc.)
In skillet heat:
3 tablespoons oil
Drop batter in to form patties
about 4 inches in diameter.
Brown on both sides, adding more
oil if needed. Garnish with
parsley sprigs. Serve for lunch,
brunch or light supper or
as a sandwich.
Makes 8-10 cakes

GOLDEN WEST SOUP

Soak overnight and drain:
1 cup dried corn kernels
1 cup garbanzo beans
Cook until tender in:
3 quarts water
1 3-pound chicken
Remove, cool and dice meat;
reserve.
To broth add:
soaked corn kernels and
garbanzo beans
Bring to boil, cover and
simmer 2 hours. Then add:
1 onion, diced
1 cup celery and some tops,
   chopped
1-1/2 cups diced carrots
1 red bell pepper, diced
1 teaspoon each salt, sugar
   and oregano
2 peppercorns
1 bay leaf
1/8 teaspoon cayenne pepper
2 tablespoons minced parsley
Bring back to boil, cover and
simmer 20 minutes or until
vegetables are just tender.
Add reserved chicken, reheat
and serve with Sourdough Bread
(page 9). Pass grated
Cheddar cheese.
Serves 6-8

POOR MAN'S STEW

Combine:
1/4 pound meaty salt pork,
   rinsed and diced
3 cups water
1/2 teaspoon each celery
   seed and mace
3/4 teaspoon thyme or marjoram
4 whole cloves
4 peppercorns
Bring to boil, cover and
simmer 30 minutes. Then add
and cook 5 minutes:
1 cup each diced carrots,
   parsnips and rutabagas
Add and cook 10 minutes:
1/2 cup diced onion
2 new potatoes, diced
1/4 cup minced parsley
Add and simmer 5 minutes:
1 teaspoon vinegar
2/3 cup crushed unsalted
   soda crackers or wafers
Adjust seasonings with salt
and pepper and serve with Sourdough Bread (page 9).
Serves 4-6

SALMON ROE

Remove roe from membrane, salt lightly and serve on melba toast with lemon wedges.

MOOSE JERKY

Cut moose steak at a 45° angle to the grain, 1/16-inch thick. Salt and pepper the strips and press to flatten with side of knife. Put a toothpick through one end and hang each on oven rack. Bake in a 140° oven, with door open 2 inches, for 8-12 hours. Store in capped jars.

SOURDOUGH PANCAKES OR WAFFLES

Combine:
1/2 cup Sourdough Starter
   (page 9)
1 cup each lukewarm water and
   evaporated milk
1-1/2 to 2 cups unbleached flour
Cover with tea towel and let stand at room temperature overnight.
In the morning beat together:
2 eggs
2 tablespoons sugar
1/2 teaspoon salt
1/2 - 1 teaspoon baking soda
(If starter is very sour use the larger proportion.)

Gently stir into starter mixture and fry as pancakes in a small amount of oil, lard or butter. For waffles add to batter with eggs:
2 tablespoons cooking oil
Serves 4

CRANBERRY SYRUP

Combine:
4 cups cranberries
1 cup brown sugar
1-1/2 cups water
1/2 cup maple syrup
Bring to boil and cook until cranberry skins pop. Serve with Sourdough Pancakes or Waffles and butter.

OCEANIA

WHEN Polynesia's first settlers from Asia stepped out of their outrigger dugouts on Samoa, Bora Bora, Tahiti and Hawaii, they found breadfruit, coconut palms, taro root and sugarcane awaiting them. Seafood was plentiful, and they brought their own pigs. Later waves of European and Asian settlers brought their own favorite foods, too, especially to Hawaii where today there's a melange of barbecued pig, poi, corned beef, chowder, stir-fried vegetables, mung beans, *teriyaki*, scones and *sashimi*.

People from all over the earth have been attracted to the 30,000 "south sea" islands, tips of a sunken continent once joined to Southeast Asia and Australia. Polynesia, Micronesia, Melanesia, Indonesia, Malaysia and the Philippines do offer intriguing indigenous foods, some at their best *au naturel*, others requiring elaborate preparation.

For the agile eater willing to clamber up a hundred-foot palm tree (or possessing a trained monkey on a rope) there are green coconuts soft enough to eat with a spoon or a toddy of palm blossom sap full of zip after a few days in the sun.

In typical imaginative fashion the Spanish named these large seeds "coconuts" because of their eyes-and-mouth markings (from "coco" meaning bugbear for frightening small children). Together with its trees the coconut has provided not only food, but also clothing, housing, heat, light, seives, rope, mats, hats, baskets and hair oil. Its juicy meat—not its thirst-quenching water—is called the tropical cow, for when grated in a few drops of water and squeezed it produces "cream." Subsequent squeezings with more water produce "milk" for soups, sauces and doughs, or for boiling vegetables, meat and seafood. With chopped turtle meat and spices the milk makes Balinese *saté* for barbecuing. It's an ideal medium for blending chilis and spices. Dried and grated or crushed for its oil, coconut meat is a versatile food.

Both the large round starchy breadfruit and the purple taro bulb can be pounded into *poi* (a word originally designating the pounding process rather than the finished dish) as can other fruits and vegetables too tough to be eaten whole. The islanders became expert pit roasters and leaf steamers. Roasting a whole pig among hot rocks for five hours in an underground oven or *imu* produces crumbly, tender, juicy pork to be eaten with *poi* and *luau* (chopped taro leaves and octopus, or chicken cooked with coconut cream) or *laulau* (chunks of meat and chopped taro leaves wrapped in *ti* leaves and steamed in a dry oven for hours). Like corn in its husks roasted over charcoal, ti leaves provide moisture for steam and their own faint aroma and flavor.

A hundred years ago Hawaiians thought white men were foolish to bring their New England salt cod and dried beef to islands with plenty of *mahi-mahi* and pigs, yet later they developed their own delicious dried salmon, *lomi lomi*, and dried meat, *pipikaula*, for feast accompaniments. On smaller islands like Samoa with fewer outsiders, natives have retained older foods like roasted breadfruit, *huapia* (coconut milk and arrowroot pudding), *se'a* (edible sea slug), eel or octopus in coconut milk, strong-flavored giant clams, and *palolo* (caviar-like sea creatures' eggs fried in butter with onions).

Food was no problem when Tahitians welcomed Europeans in 1767, but when the French took over in 1842 their already good gastronomy became even better. Maybe it's better to say broader, for even with newly introduced techniques and garlic it was hard to beat *e'ia ota*, or *poisson cru*—raw fish, tuna "cooked" in lime juice and salt, then soaked and served in coconut milk to relieve the acid bite.

In the Philippines Spaniards left their mark in *pochido* (from *cocido*), cooking with lard, and tempering the fiery foods of the Indies. Still the sour *sinigang* (a meat and tomato soup with vegetables and sour fruits) and salty *bagoongs* or *patis* (concentrated fish sauces) are a far cry from the food of Madrid. So is the light, white cheese of *carbao* (water buffalo) milk and *adobo*, a complicated, thick, garlicky stew. The peasants of Luzon terraced mountains into steps to grow rice as did their ancestors on lowland deltas along the rivers of Southeast Asia.

Malaysia and Indonesia were commercially active long before the Portuguese, Spanish and Dutch ruthlessly took over; thus the foods of the South China Sea community are unusually complex. Here diverse peoples have always used nutmeg, cloves and mace from the Moluccas, pepper from Java, ginger and turmeric from India, Chinese cinnamon or *cassia* from Sumatra, and true cinnamon, more delicate and subtle, from Ceylon.

Java has its *sambal*, a chili relish with garlic, shallots and lime juice; with the addition of the acid *tamarind* pulp, *lado* is made for stir frying with seafood, vegetables or eggs. *Sago* flour from the inner pulp of the *sago* palm makes a soft dough, *popeda*, for plopping into vegetable soup and slurping as best one can without a spoon. The widely popular, everyday dish called *gulai* is a curry-like dish with coconut milk. For jungle trips in Sumatra there are *rendang* (spiced beef chunks cooked in coconut milk until all moisture evaporates) or *lontong* (rolls of rice steamed in banana leaves), both of which keep for days.

It's rice, of course, prepared in thousands of ways, that provides the most sustenance for teeming millions in the true Indies. Starting in the Orient, rice has literally circled the globe, moving Westward with Arab traders to the Mediterranean, and then across the Atlantic with Spanish and Portuguese colonizers to the Caribbean. In the late 1600's it was introduced in South Carolina and shortly after in Georgia. In 1901 the Kyushu strain made large-scale growing practical in Texas, because it withstood hurricanes; in 1916 other varieties took hold in the dry heat of California's Sacramento valley. The circle has now been completed by western science's development of a new super-rice, IR-8, which can dramatically increase the yield where it's needed most: in the Far East, where rice growing has scarcely changed in a thousand years. At this point IR-8 has one fatal flaw: it contains so much amylose, a starch component which forms a hard gel at ordinary temperatures, that its grains won't stick together like old-style glutinous rice. Rice eaters in the Orient refuse to accept it, especially field workers accustomed to portable lunches of cold rice balls.

During the past twenty years Thailand has been yielding archeological secrets that raise exciting new theories. Thailand, not Kurdistan, may have been civilization's true cradle. Mounting evidence indicates that ancient peoples here made pottery, manufactured stone tools and cast bronze, thousands of years earlier than in the Near East, India or China. Using radioactive techniques scientists have proven that beans were grown as a crop in Thailand at least as far back as 9500 B.C., two thousand years earlier than cereal grain cultivation in Iran. Rice culture in Thailand dates from 5500 years ago, some 1500 years earlier than previously assumed for India. Perhaps naming Southeast Asia "Indo-China" for the Indian and Chinese cultures that supposedly shaped its history will prove to be our most basic anthropological error to date. Maybe a modern explorer of the past will come up with a special name uniquely designating Thailand as the source of culture—as the starting point where clever navigators as early as 4,000 B.C. set sail for Japan, Taiwan, East Africa, the Mediterranean and Indonesia in outrigger canoes provisioned with beans and rice.

HAWAII/TAHITI

CHICKEN AND SPINACH IN COCONUT MILK

Brown on all sides in:
3 tablespoons butter or
    rendered chicken fat (page 17)
1 3-pound chicken, cut up
Lower heat, cover and simmer
in own juices 10 minutes.
Then add:
1 cup coconut milk (page 17)
Place on top of chicken:
1 bunch fresh spinach leaves,
    cut in half
Cover and simmer 15 minutes.
Salt and pepper to taste.
Bind (page 17) and serve with
plain boiled rice.
Serves 4

LOMI SALMON
Marinated Salmon Appetizer

Cut into small bite-size pieces:
1 pound fresh salmon fillets
Sprinkle with:
1/3 cup coarse sea salt
Pour over salmon and toss
lightly:
1/4 cup fresh lemon juice
Cover and refrigerate 8 hours.
(Do not use metal container.)

MAHI-MAHI

Cut into cubes:
2 pounds Mahi-Mahi (Blue
    Pacific Dolphin) steaks
Place on skewers alternately
with:
fresh pineapple chunks
Brush with mixture of:
1/4 cup lemon juice
2 tablespoons each soy sauce
    and peanut oil
1 tablespoon sugar
Broil over hot coals 2-5 minutes.
Do not overcook.
Serves 4

POISSON CRU
Marinated Raw Fish

Cut into bite-size pieces:
1 pound fresh raw fish
Combine for marinade:
1/2 cup coconut milk (page 17)
1-1/2 teaspoons sea salt
1/3 teaspoon finely minced garlic
1/4 cup minced green onions
1/3 cup lime juice
Toss fish in marinade and
marinate 8 hours.

SINIGANG
Tomato Soup

Combine:
2 quarts water
2 fresh pork hocks, blanched
    (page 17) 5 minutes and rinsed
1 tablespoon Patis*
2 tablespoons tamarind juice*
Bring to gentle boil, cover and
simmer 1-1/2 hours until pork
hocks are tender. Remove pork
hocks, dice meat and return to
soup. Then add:
2 onions, cut in chunks
3 ripe tomatoes, quartered
Cook 30 minutes. Can also add
vegetables such as bok choy,
mustard greens, cabbage or
bitter melon.
Serves 6

QUINISANG NEMBO
Mung Bean Soup

Soak at least 2 hours:
1 cup mung beans*
Remove skins and combine with:
6 cups chicken stock
2 tablespoons dried shrimp*
1/2 cup chopped tomatoes
1 garlic clove, minced
1 onion, diced
1 teaspoon oil
1 tablespoon tamarind juice*
Bring to gentle boil, cover
and simmer 40 minutes.
Serves 6

VEGETABLE SALAD

Arrange on platter sliced
tomatoes, cucumbers and
hard-cooked Hom Dahn (page 25).
Serve with a sprinkling of salt.

FRUIT SALAD

Dress fresh fruits such as
mangoes, papayas, pineapple,
peaches, bananas, avocados with
lemon or lime juice and sugar
to taste.

CHAMPORODI
Rice Pudding

This is eaten for breakfast
or as an afternoon snack.
Combine and cook, uncovered, over
medium heat, stirring to prevent
sticking, for 30 minutes:
1/2 cup malagkit (sweet rice,
    also called glutinous), washed
    and drained
2 cups coconut milk (page 17)
Add and mix well:
1 ounce bitter chocolate,
    melted
1/4 cup sugar
Cook over low heat 5 minutes.
Remove from heat and add:
1/2 cup evaporated milk
Pour into individual bowls and
serve hot or cold, with cream if
desired.
Serves 4

PHILIPPINES

APA
Deep-Fried Rolled Lumpia

Sauté until transparent in:
2 tablespoons oil
1 onion, diced
2 garlic cloves, minced
Add and cook, stirring
frequently, until moisture
evaporates:
3/4 pound ground beef
1/2 pound chorizo sausage meat
1 bay leaf, crushed
1 cup diced tomatoes
1/2 cup each raisins and cooked
    garbanzo beans
Cool. Prepare:
24 lumpia wrappers**
Place 2 tablespoons filling
onto each wrapper. Fold over
once, then fold in sides and roll.
Deep fry immediately, seam side
down, until golden. Drain and
serve with lettuce dressed with
garlic, vinegar, salt and pepper.
Makes 24

APA
Open Lumpia

Sauté until transparent in:
2 tablespoons oil
1 onion, thinly sliced
1 garlic clove, minced
Add, cover and cook 10 minutes:
1/2 pound each diced chicken,
    pork and ham
1 tablespoon each soy sauce
    and sugar
1/2 cup chicken broth
Add and cook 3 minutes:
1/2 pound raw shrimp
Prepare and deep fry:
 lumpia wrappers**
Place on each wrapper:
1 lettuce leaf
Fill with meat mixture.
Pass bowls of any combination of
these fillings:
diced bean curd*
shredded Chinese cabbage
cooked garbanzo beans, potatoes,
    lima beans, and/or green beans
shredded carrots
diced hearts of palm
pimientos
Serves 6

**Lumpia wrappers are available
in Philippine stores in 1-pound
packages containing 24 9-inch
rounds. If frozen defrost in
refrigerator overnight before
using. If unable to obtain, mix
well 2 cups each water and
unbleached flour. Heat a 7-inch
crêpe pan and brush with oil to
cover. Brush batter onto hot pan
evenly and thinly (pan should
not be too hot); cook over
moderate heat till set; turn and
cook other side. If crêpe pan
is properly seasoned it will not
need more oil. This amount
makes 24 rounds.

GINESA
Vegetable Dish

Brown in:
1 tablespoon rendered pork fat
    (page 17)
1/2 pound pork, cut in 1/2-inch
    dice
1 onion, diced
1 garlic clove, minced
1/2 bell pepper, diced
Add and brown 2 minutes:
1/2 pound raw shrimp
Add:
1 teaspoon each shrimp paste*
    and Patis*
2 ripe tomatoes, quartered
1 pound any vegetable such as:
string or long beans
okra
cabbage
chayote
cauliflower
Cover and steam until vegetables
are just tender-crisp, about
5 minutes. Season to taste with
salt and pepper.
Serves 4

ADOBO
Meat Dish

Combine:
1 frying chicken, cut up
1 pound pork, cut into 1-inch
    pieces
1/2 cup each vinegar and water
1 bay leaf
1/2 teaspoon black pepper
2 garlic cloves, minced
Bring to gentle boil, cover and
cook over medium heat 30 minutes
or until tender. Remove cover,
turn up heat and cook to
evaporate liquid. Then add:
2 tablespoons oil
Brown chicken and pork lightly,
transfer to heated serving dish
and deglaze (page 17) with 1/4 cup
water. Pour over chicken and pork
and serve with plain rice.
Serves 4-6

INEHOW
Baked Milk Fish

Sauté 5 minutes in:
1 tablespoon oil
1 onion, chopped
1 garlic clove, minced
Add:
1 cup each cooked rice and
    chopped tomatoes
1 teaspoon Patis*
1/4 teaspoon black pepper
Salt inside and out:
1 whole bangus**,
    about 3 pounds
Stuff with rice mixture, rub
both sides with oil and arrange
lemon slices on top of fish.
Wrap securely in banana leaves
or heavy foil. Bake in a 375°
oven 20 minutes for first pound,
10 minutes for each additional
pound.
Serves 4-6

**Bangus is available frozen
in Philippine stores; it is
especially good because of
the flavorful fat in the lining of
the stomach. Substitute sea bass,
carp or rock cod.

PHILIPPINES

ESCABECHE WITH PAPAYA
Fried Fish with Papaya Sauce

Prepare:
Sweet and Sour Sauce (page 27)
To sauce add:
1 teaspoon minced browned garlic
minced hot chili peppers to taste (page 17)
1-2 green papayas, thinly sliced
Cook 10 minutes or until papayas are tender. Serve on any fried whole fish.

PANCIT MOLO
Filled Noodle Dumpling

Combine:
1 cup ground pork
1/2 cup each ground chicken and shrimp
1 egg, beaten
1/4 cup each minced onion and bamboo shoots
3 tablespoons each minced green pepper and chopped water chestnuts
1 teaspoon minced garlic
1/2 teaspoon salt
1/4 teaspoon black pepper
Set aside half above mixture and with remainder fill **molo (wonton) skins** (page 12). Place a teaspoon of filling on each skin, wet edges of skin and fold over to make a triangle. Press edges firmly and set aside.

Brown in:
3 tablespoons oil
1/2 cup minced onion
2 teaspoons minced garlic
Add and brown:
reserved stuffing
Add, bring to boil and simmer 10 minutes:
8 cups chicken stock
Drop molos into boiling salted water and cook 4-5 minutes until they rise to surface. Remove with slotted spoon and add to soup. Garnish with chopped green onions and serve immediately.
Serves 8

PANCIT LUGLUG PALABOK
Rice Noodles with Sauce

Pork Sauce
Brown in:
1 tablespoon oil
**4-6 garlic cloves, finely
minced**
Remove and set aside.
In same pan brown:
1/2 pound ground pork
Add, cover, bring to gentle
boil and cook 5 minutes:
1/2 pound raw shrimp
1/2 pound bean curd*, cubed
1/2 cup shrimp juice**
1 tablespoon Patis*
Adjust seasonings with salt
and pepper and keep warm.

Red Sauce
Soak 30 minutes in:
1/2 cup warm water
1 teaspoon achiote seeds*
Sieve, press out color, discard
seeds and combine liquid with:
1-1/2 cups shrimp juice
3 tablespoons flour
Stir and cook until smooth
and thickened. Keep warm.

Soak 10 minutes in cold water
to soften:
1 8-ounce package Bijon*
(Luglug) noodles
Bring to a boil and cook
2 minutes:
8 cups boiling salted water
drained Bijon noodles
Drain and place on heated
serving platter. Cover with
the red sauce, top with pork
sauce and sprinkle with:
reserved garlic
cracklings pounded into
powder form
finely flaked smoked fish
Garnish with any
combination of:
chopped hard-cooked eggs
chopped celery leaves
chopped green onion
shredded lettuce
lemon wedges
Serves 4-6

**Shrimp juice can be made by
pounding shrimp shells, heads
and tails in a mortar and
pestle, covering with boiling
water and boiling 5 minutes,
and then straining. If unable
to buy shrimp with shells,
substitute clam juice.

HALO-HALO
Fruit Dessert

In a tall glass place a layer
of shaved ice. Top with:
halo-halo ** or any combination
of
kaong (sugar palm)
red mango
macapuno (coconut sport)
halaya ube (yam jam)
sweet beans (white bean)
nata de piña (gelatinous
pineapple mold)
nata de coco (gelatinous)
coconut mold)
garbanzo beans
langka (sweet jackfruit)
Add another layer of shaved ice
and top with evaporated milk or
ice cream.
**combination of fruits
available in cans in Philippine
stores

AJAM SATAY
Marinated Chicken Barbecue

Purée in blender:
2 onions, cut up
2 hot red chilis (page 17),
    cut up
2 garlic cloves
1 tablespoon chopped fresh
    ginger root
1 teaspoon shrimp paste*
1 stick dried sereh** or
    1/2 teaspoon sereh powder
2 tablespoons each peanut
    butter and tamarind juice*
2 teaspoons sugar
1 teaspoon salt
1/2 cup each water and
    peanut oil
Marinate in above mixture
1 hour:
2 fryers, cut up
Broil over hot coals. turning
frequently, 10 minutes per side
or until tender. Serve with
fresh sliced bananas and
pineapple.
Serves 6-8

**lemon grass sold in Middle
    Eastern or Indonesian shops

NASI GORING
Rice with Curry Sauce

Brown in:
1/4 cup peanut oil
1-1/2 cups each white and
    brown rice, washed and
    drained
1 onion, minced
1 red or green bell pepper,
    minced
Add:
5 cups stock or water
Bring to gentle boil and cook
until all water evaporates.
Reduce heat to simmer, cover and
cook 30 minutes until rice
is tender.

Curry Sauce
Cook and stir until bubbly:
3 tablespoons butter or
    peanut oil
2 tablespoons curry powder
Add to make a paste:
1 teaspoon lime juice
4 tablespoons flour
Gradually add:
1-1/2 cups chicken stock,
    coconut milk (page 17), half-
    and-half cream or combination

Cook and stir until smooth and
thickened. Thin to desired
consistency and add:
1-1/2 tablespoons peanut butter
1/4 teaspoon grated fresh
    ginger root
Keep warm in double boiler.
Mound rice on heated platter and
arrange around it:
3 cups cooked diced chicken
    or shrimp
Top with Egg Garni (page 16)
and garnish with watercress.
Around the platter serve
a choice of the following
condiments:
mango or peach chutney
shredded coconut* browned
    in oven
chopped unsalted freshly
    roasted peanuts
chopped onions and plumped
    raisins (page 17) sautéed
    lightly in butter
finger lengths of peeled
    cucumber (a must)
fried or baked plantains* or
    bananas, cubed
krupuk (shrimp chips*)
slivered pickled red ginger*
finely minced chili peppers
    (page 17)
Pass the curry sauce.
Serves 8-10

BEEF SATE
Skewered Beef

Purée in blender:
1/4 cup each salad oil, lemon
    juice and soy sauce
2 garlic cloves
1 large onion, cut up
2 hot red chilis (page 17),
    cut up
3 tablespoons chopped
    fresh coriander*
1/4 cup roasted peanuts
1 teaspoon sesame oil*
2 tablespoons brown sugar
1/2 teaspoon black pepper
Marinate in above mixture
2 hours:
3 pounds beef sirloin, cut in
    1-inch cubes
Skewer and broil over hot coals,
turning frequently, 5-7 minutes.
Serve with rice and Bean Sprout
and Cucumber Salad.
Pass a dip of:
2/3 cup soy sauce
1 tablespoon each dark molasses
    and light brown sugar
Serves 6

BEAN SPROUT AND
CUCUMBER SALAD

Combine:
1 pound fresh bean sprouts
2 cucumbers, seeded and cut
    in julienne*
1/2 cup chopped green onions
Toss with dressing of:
1/2 cup white vinegar
2 tablespoons sugar
1 teaspoon salt
Serve on lettuce leaves and top
with unsalted toasted chopped
peanuts.
Serves 6

MANGO CHUTNEY

Place in large pot:
1 onion, minced
1/2 pound raisins
2 garlic cloves, minced
3/4 cup fresh ginger root,
    chopped
2 small red chilis (page 17),
    chopped
1 tablespoon each salt and
    whole cloves
1 quart cider vinegar
3 cups brown sugar
5 pounds mangoes, peeled
    and sliced
Bring to boil over high heat,
reduce heat to medium and cook
1 hour until thick. Pour into
4 hot, sterilized pint jars.
Seal.

For peach chutney
Substitute peaches for mangoes,
omit cloves and add:
2 tablespoons mustard seeds

THAILAND

CHICKEN SALAD

Marinate 30 minutes:
2 pounds chicken breasts, split
1 tablespoon each hoisin sauce*,
**   soy sauce and sherry**
Brown on all sides in oil,
cover and cook 15 minutes until
chicken is tender but still
juicy. Cool and shred chicken
meat with fingers into long
strands; cut crispy skin in
julienne*
Combine chicken meat and
skin with:
2 tablespoons hoisin sauce
1 teaspoon sesame oil*
1/4 cup lemon juice
2 tablespoons each chopped fresh
**   roasted peanuts and toasted**
**   sesame seeds**
1/4 cup each slivered green
**   onions and fresh coriander**
**   leaves***

Toss lightly with two-thirds of the:
fried py mei fun (see below)
and serve on a bed of:
lettuce leaves
with the remaining py mei fun
sprinkled on top. Surround with:
fried shrimp chips*
To deep fry py mei fun*
Break up 1/4 pound noodles and
drop by small handfuls into hot
corn oil (at least 1/2-inch
deep); fry until golden.
They will expand 10 times their
original size. Remove
immediately and drain on paper
toweling; repeat with remaining
noodles; do not overcrowd.
Shrimp chips are deep fried
in the same way.
Serves 4-6

DOM YAM KOONG
Lemon Shrimp Soup

Shell (reserve shells) and
devein:
1 pound raw shrimp
Set aside.
Combine:
reserved shrimp shells
6 cups water
1 garlic clove
1/2 lemon
1 bay leaf
1/2 teaspoon coriander seeds
1 hot red chili pepper (page 17),
**   cut up**
1 teaspoon each salt and
**   fish soy***
Bring to gentle boil, cover
and simmer 30 minutes. Strain.
Soak 10 minutes, drain and cut
in thirds:
4 ounces bean thread noodles*
Bring stock to boil and add
noodles. Bring back to boil
and cook 5 minu
reserved shrimp
Bring back to boil and cook
2 minutes or until shrimp are
just tender; do not overcook.
Garnish each bowl of soup with
chopped green onions and
a slice of lemon.
Serves 6

✳ GLOSSARY

- **ACHIOTE OIL (ANNATTO)** Heat 2 tablespoons achiote seeds (small, red seeds used for color and delicate flavor; available in Puerto Rican and Mexican markets*) and 1/3 cup oil or lard until bubbly. Strain; reserve seeds for reuse.
- **AGAR-AGAR** See **KANTEN**.
- **AJI OIL** Chili oil; sesame oil with cayenne pepper. Available in Oriental markets.*
- **AJI PEPPERS** Small yellow peppers, 2 inches long, and very hot. When old turn red and hotter. See page 17 for handling directions.
- **AKAMISO** See **MISO**.
- **APIO** Starchy root vegetable, seasonal. Sold in Latin American markets.
- **AZUKI** Canned, small sweetened red beans, sold in Oriental markets.* May be prepared by using dried azuki beans and cooking until soft and mashing with sugar to taste.
- **BEAN CURD** Fresh bean cakes (not paste), made of puréed soybeans pressed into cakes; also called tofu. Sold in Oriental and some super-markets. Instant and canned available.*

- **BEAN THREAD NOODLES** Also called peastarch, shining, cellophane and transparent noodles. Opaque fine white noodle made from ground mung peas. Sold in coiled bundles by weight in Oriental markets.*
- **BIJON NOODLE** Sometimes called **Luglug**, thicker version of rice noodle available in Philippine stores. Substitute any rice noodle such as **py mei fun**.*
- **BONITO FLAKES, DRIED** Dried fish flakes sold by weight in Oriental markets.*
- **CHINESE CHIVES** Flat-leafed chive with slight garlic flavor, sold in Oriental markets. Easily grown from seed.
- **CHINESE PARSLEY** Delicate parsley, with slightly pungent flavor, aromatic and distinct. Easily grown from seed. Called coriander in Middle and Far Eastern countries, cilantro in Spanish-speaking countries.
- **CHINESE SAUSAGE** Lop Chiang, sweet pork sausage sold in Oriental markets.
- **CHINESE TURNIPS** Long white radish, more delicate in flavor than the round variety. Sold in Oriental markets.

- **CILANTRO** See **CHINESE PARSLEY**.
- **COCONUT, DRIED** Shredded, unsweetened coconut sold in natural food stores.
- **CORIANDER, FRESH** See **CHINESE PARSLEY**.
- **DAIKON** Japanese white radish, sold in Oriental markets.
- **DOW SEE** Fermented, salted, black beans used only for flavoring, sold in Oriental markets.*
- **FISH SOY OR PATIS** Water extract of fish and salt, used for flavoring; more subtle when used in cooking than the unpleasant smell may indicate. Sold in Oriental and Philippine markets.*
- **"5" SPICE POWDER** Blend of cloves, fennel, cinnamon, ginger, star anise and sugar; sold in Oriental markets.*
- **GREEN TEA POWDER** Powdered green tea, also used in Japanese tea ceremony; sold in Oriental markets.*

GLOSSARY

- **HOISIN SAUCE** Thick dark sauce of soybeans, chili spices and garlic. Sold in Oriental markets.*
- **ITALIAN PARSLEY** Broad, flat-leafed parsley with a more concentrated flavor. Easily grown from seed.
- **JAGGARY** Form of raw brown sugar, sold in East Indian or specialty markets. Substitute 3/4 cup dark brown sugar to 1 tablespoon dark molasses.
- **JULIENNE** Food cut into match-like strips.
- **KANTEN** Shirokaku (white) or akakaku (red); also called agar-agar. Used like gelatin for thickening Oriental desserts; sold by weight in Oriental markets.*
- **KATSUOBUSHI** See **BONITO FLAKES**.
- **KOMBU** Dried sheet kelp (seaweed) for dashi; sold in Japanese markets.*
- **LARD, PORK** Used in Latin American cooking; superior flavor. Cut pork fat back into small pieces, cover with water and simmer until fat bits are very soft. Sieve through medium strainer, forcing half of the fat through.

Cool and refrigerate. Pure lard will rise to top; remove and wrap to store in refrigerator.
- **MALANGA or ELEPHANT EARS** Leaf of taro root. Sold in Puerto Rican or Mexican markets.
- **MANIOC FLOUR** Ground cassava; lends texture, widely used in Brazil as we use grated Parmesan cheese. Sold in specialty markets. Substitute farina.
- **MATSUBA** Japanese leafy herb, large leafed; looks like parsley family. Distinct flavor, easily grown from seed.
- **MIRIN** Sweet Japanese wine used in cooking; sold in Oriental and many supermarkets. Substitute sherry with a little sugar.
- **MISO** Fermented paste of malt, salt and soy beans. Sold in Oriental markets as akamiso (red) or shirumiso (white).*
- **MUNG BEANS** Small pea bean sold in Oriental or natural food stores*; also used for sprouting bean sprouts.
- **MUSHROOMS, DRIED FOREST** Black (winter) mushrooms with distinct flavor; sold in Oriental markets.*
- **NORI** Sheet seaweed sold in Oriental markets.*

- **OYSTER SAUCE** Thick oyster-flavored sauce sold in Oriental markets.*
- **PARSLEY ROOT** Hamburg or turnip rooted parsley used to flavor soups and stews. Easily grown from seed.
- **PATIS** See **FISH SOY**.
- **PECORINO CHEESE** Italian sheep's milk cheese used like Parmesan; sold in Italian delicatessens.
- **PICKLED RED GINGER or YOSABURO ZUKE** Ginger pickled in vinegar brine; sold in Oriental markets.*
- **PLANTAINS or PLATANOS** Starchy vegetable that looks like a large banana and is used green or ripe in cooking; sold in Puerto Rican and Mexican markets.
- **PLUM SAUCE** Thick sauce of plums, chili and spices similar to a fruit chutney. Especially good with roast duck or other game or poultry. Ready to eat, sold in Oriental markets.*

184

• **PRESERVED MIXED-VEGETABLE RELISH** Sweet shredded cucumber and carrot. Sold canned in Oriental markets.*

• **PY MEI FUN** Fine rice sticks sold in Oriental markets.*

• **RICE VINEGAR** Special vinegar sold in Oriental and some supermarkets*, milder in flavor.

• **SAKE** Japanese rice wine sold in Oriental and some super-markets. Substitute dry sherry or white wine.

• **SESAME OIL** Made from toasted seeds, golden brown in color and strong in flavor; more an extract than an oil. Sold in Oriental and some super-markets.*

• **SHINGIKU** Fresh chrysanthemum leaves; sold in Japanese markets.

• **SHIRUMISO** See MISO.

• **SHRIMP CHIPS** Krupuk in Indonesia; pappadoms in India; sold in Oriental markets* and used in Far Eastern countries. Deep fry in hot oil just until chips puff. Drain on paper toweling.

• **SHRIMP, DRIED** Tiny dried shrimp with concentrated flavor. Sold by weight in Oriental markets.*

• **SHRIMP PASTE** Fermented shrimp sauce with strong unpleasant odor and a subtle taste when added to foods. Closest substitue is anchovy paste, but flavor is not authentic. Sold in Oriental and Philippine markets.*

• **SOBA** Buckwheat noodle sold in Oriental markets.* Chasoba has green tea powder added.

• **STAR ANISE SEED** Dried star anise with distinct licorice flavor. Sold in Chinese markets.*

• **TAHINA** Sesame paste sold in Middle Eastern specialty shops.

• **TAMARIND JUICE** Pour 1/2 cup boiling water over 2 tablespoons dried pulp of tamarind (available in Philippine markets and Latin American local stores). Mix well and press through sieve to extract juice. One tablespoon lemon rind and 2 tablespoons lemon juice may be substituted for 2 tablespoons tamarind juice (not the authentic flavor, however).

• **TANGERINE PEEL (GWA PEI)** Dried tangerine, mandarin orange or orange peel, concentrated flavor. Sold by weight in Oriental markets.*

• **TURNIP GREENS (CHOONG TOY)** Turnips and tops preserved with salt, dried and rolled; not to be confused with dried turnips. Sold in Oriental markets.*

• **UDON** Japanese wheat noodle, sold in Oriental markets.*

• **WASABI** Green horseradish powder sold in Oriental markets.*

• **WONDRA FLOUR** Closest to Czechoslovakian flour.

• **YAUTIAS** Starchy root vegetable of taro root family; sold in Latin American markets.

• **YELLOW MUNG DAL** Dried mung beans sold in East Indian or natural food stores. Dal means bean has been split and skin removed.

*If unable to obtain write P.O. Box 1074, San Rafael, California 94901 for mail-order price list.

INDEX

INDEX

INDEX

This book is printed on 100 percent recycled paper.

BIOGRAPHICAL DATA

In an earlier 101 Production with the deceivingly simple title "Soup" Coralie Castle proved her prowess in the kitchen by presenting scores of original recipes for soups from all over the world with widely varied ingredients and seasonings.

At an early age Mrs. Castle learned to cook German-American specialties in her mother's kitchen, and over the years built up a general fund of recipes and techniques. San Francisco's array of international cuisines inspired her to explore and experiment in earnest, to develop her own versions of famous dishes of all kinds as well as devise completely new ones.

Margaret Lee Gin's culinary background is distinctly unusual. At home young Li Tuey (her Chinese name) mastered stir-fried Cantonese delicacies, spicy hot Mexican dishes and apple pie, for her parents grew up in

Canton, settled in Tucson and owned a grocery store featuring homemade American pastry. An expert seamstress, she learned costume designing, which eventually led to a line of ski clothes in San Francisco. A young, free-lance commercial artist named William Gin was her catalog illustrator.

Margaret Lee's Telegraph Hill apartment became the site of many an Oriental feast for large gatherings of her friends. After marriage to William Gin and two sons, Mrs. Gin still continued to gain new admirers of her culinary skills. Friends persuaded her to teach Chinese cooking classes, which Mrs. Castle, in the midst of writing "Soup," eagerly attended to expand her knowledge of soups.

As these two creative cooks became acquainted, sparks began to fly, for each acted as a catalyst on the other. Their husbands

became involved, too, believing that historical peasant foods of the world could appeal to both modern gourmet cooks and the growing number of people who want inexpensive, tasty, nourishing foods.

Coralie Castle and Margaret Gin proceeded to explore over a thousand recipes. Meanwhile William Gin investigated peasant life from the visual standpoint and Alfred Castle undertook extensive research on the culinary history of the world. Ethnic experts in the San Francisco area cooperated by sharing food ideas from their ancestral or their personal experience.

After months of testing and changing to meet critical standards, the authors narrowed potential dishes down to the several hundred contained in this book.